WORLD HISTORY SERIES ■■■

The Ancient Near East

Titles in the World History Series

WORLD HISTORY SERIES ■■■

The Ancient Near East

by
Clarice Swisher

935
swi

Lucent Books, P.O. Box 289011, San Diego, CA 92198-9011

Library of Congress Cataloging-in-Publication Data

Swisher, Clarice, 1933–
    The Ancient Near East / by Clarice Swisher
        p. cm.—(World history series)
    Includes bibliographical references and index.
    ISBN 1-56006-284-3
    1. Iraq—History—To 634—Juvenile literature [1. Iraq—
History—To 634.]   I.Title. II. Series.
DS71.S95   1995
935—dc20   94-37173
                                                          CIP
                                                           AC

For Karen

Acknowledgments

I am grateful to many people who have given me generous help and support during the research for and writing of this book. In particular, I thank Douglas Schaffer, a first reader, who offered many opinions and helpful suggestions. At the time of the writing, Douglas Schaffer was finishing his seventh grade in school. Among other things, his comments helped determine when explanations were clear and what words needed defining.

Contents

Foreword

Each year on the first day of school, nearly every history teacher faces the task of explaining why his or her students should study history. One logical answer to this question is that exploring what happened in our past explains how the things we often take for granted—our customs, ideas, and institutions—came to be. As statesman and historian Winston Churchill put it, "Every nation or group of nations has its own tale to tell. Knowledge of the trials and struggles is necessary to all who would comprehend the problems, perils, challenges, and opportunities which confront us today." Thus, a study of history puts modern ideas and institutions in perspective. For example, though the founders of the United States were talented and creative thinkers, they clearly did not invent the concept of democracy. Instead, they adapted some democratic ideas that had originated in ancient Greece and with which the Romans, the British, and others had experimented. An exploration of these cultures, then, reveals their very real connection to us through institutions that continue to shape our daily lives.

Another reason often given for studying history is the idea that lessons exist in the past from which contemporary societies can benefit and learn. This idea, although controversial, has always been an intriguing one for historians. Those that agree that society can benefit from the past often quote philosopher George Santayana's famous statement, "Those who cannot remember the past are condemned to repeat it." Historians who ascribe to Santayana's philosophy believe that, for

example, studying the events that led up to the major world wars or other significant historical events would allow society to chart a different and more favorable course in the future.

Just as difficult as convincing students to realize the importance of studying history is the search for useful and interesting supplementary materials that present historical events in a context that can be easily understood. The volumes in Lucent Books' World History Series attempt to present a broad, balanced, and penetrating view of the march of history. Ancient Egypt's important wars and rulers, for example, are presented against the rich and colorful backdrop of Egyptian religious, social, and cultural developments. The series engages the reader by enhancing historical events with these cultural contexts. For example, in *Ancient Greece*, the text covers the role of women in that society. Slavery is discussed in *The Roman Empire*, as well as how slaves earned their freedom. The numerous and varied aspects of everyday life in these and other societies are explored in each volume of the series. Additionally, the series covers the major political, cultural, and philosophical ideas as the torch of civilization is passed from ancient Mesopotamia and Egypt, through Greece, Rome, Medieval Europe, and other world cultures, to the modern day.

The material in the series is formatted in a thorough, precise, and organized manner. Each volume offers the reader a comprehensive and clearly written overview of an important historical event or period. The topic under discussion is placed in a broad, historical context. For example, *The Italian Renaissance* begins with a discussion of the High Middle Ages and the loss of central control that allowed certain Italian cities to develop artistically. The book ends by looking forward to the Reformation and interpreting the societal changes that grew out of the Renaissance. Thus, students are not only involved in an historical era, but also enveloped by the events leading up to that era and the events following it.

One important and unique feature in the World History Series is the primary and secondary source quotations that richly supplement each volume. These quotes are useful in a number of ways. First, they allow students access to sources they would not normally be exposed to because of the difficulty and obscurity of the original source. The quotations range from interesting anecdotes to far-sighted cultural perspectives and are drawn from historical witnesses both past and present. Second, the quotes demonstrate how and where historians themselves derive their information on the past as they strive to reach a consensus on historical events. Lastly, all of the quotes are footnoted, familiarizing students with the citation process and allowing them to verify quotes and/or look up the original source if the quote piques their interest.

Finally, the books in the World History Series provide a detailed launching point for further research. Each book contains a bibliography specifically geared toward student research. A second, annotated bibliography introduces students to all the sources the author consulted when compiling the book. A chronology of important dates gives students an overview, at a glance, of the topic covered. Where applicable, a glossary of terms is included.

In short, the series is designed not only to acquaint readers with the basics of history, but also to make them aware that their lives are a part of an ongoing human saga. Perhaps they will then come to the same realization as famed historian Arnold Toynbee. In his monumental work, *A Study of History*, he wrote about becoming aware of history flowing through him in a mighty current, and of his own life "welling like a wave in the flow of this vast tide."

Important Dates in the History of the Ancient Near East

B.C.	10,000	9500	9000	8500	8000	7500	7000	6500	6000	550

B.C.

ca. 10,000
Highland people invent agriculture and domesticate animals

ca. 6000
Semites and Highland people mix in Tigris-Euphrates valley

ca. 5500
Invention of the plow, irrigation, the wheel, and the sexagesimal number system

ca. 5000
First priests and temples

ca. 4900
First cities develop: Eridu, Ubaid, Uruk, Ur

ca. 4800
Invention of pictographs, the first writing

ca. 4500
Invention of cuneiform writing

ca. 4000
Development of city-states

ca. 2800
The Great Flood

ca. 2650
Gilgamesh becomes king of Uruk and Agga the king of Kish

ca. 2625
The First Dynasty of Ur

ca. 2500
The Epic of Gilgamesh is written

2370
Sargon, a Semite, becomes king of Sumer

2113
Ur-Nammu begins the Third Dynasty of Ur

ca. 2100
The Third Dynasty ziggurat is built; Abraham leaves Ur, settles in Hebron, and makes covenant with Yahweh to found a Hebrew nation

2006
Elamites capture Ur, ending Sumer as a nation

1792
Hammurabi becomes king of Babylon and writes laws

1750
Hammurabi dies and the Old Babylonian Empire falls

1595
Hittites conquer Babylon

1500
Kassites take control of Babylon

ca. 1300
Moses leads Hebrews out of Egypt to Mount Sinai and receives the Ten Commandments

ca. 1250
Phoenician sailors are leading traders

1171
End of Kassite empire in Babylon

ca. 1120
Nebuchadrezzar I attacks Elamites and recovers the statue of Marduk

1000
David becomes king of Judah, the Hebrew nation

910
Assyrians conquer Babylon

883
Ashurnasirpal II becomes first Assyrian monarch

744
Tiglath-pileser III becomes king and founds the Assyrian Empire

722
Assyrian army destroys the Hebrew nation of Israel

721
Sargon II becomes king of Assyria and begins building palace at Khorsabad

704
Sennacherib becomes king of Assyria and in anger destroys Babylon

668
Ashurbanipal becomes king of Assyria and creates a library in his palace

612
Assyrian Empire falls when its three main cities are destroyed

604
Nebuchadrezzar II comes to power in Babylon and rebuilds city, including hanging gardens and Tower of Babel

586
Nebuchadrezzar II destroys Jerusalem, ending the Hebrew nation

539
Persian king Cyrus conquers Babylon

520
Persian king Darius brings in new government and taxes

485
Persian king Xerxes destroys Babylon

ca. 450
Aramaic language replaces Babylonian language

ca. 350
Ur disappears under sand after Euphrates changes its course

331
Greek Alexander the Great conquers Babylon, ending the first civilization

Civilization Rises Out of the Desert

In ancient times, in the southern part of what is now Iraq, a group of people made a garden out of a desert. After centuries, this small agricultural area was named Sumer; as the culture expanded, the larger area took on other names, and today scholars refer to the Tigris-Euphrates region at the dawn of history as Mesopotamia. This culture was one of four that became great civilizations in ancient times. The other three also developed along rivers—Egypt along the Nile River, India along the Indus and Ganges Rivers, and China along the Wei and Hwang Ho Rivers. All four had many features in common, but they developed independently. Not until the twentieth century did archaeologists discover that

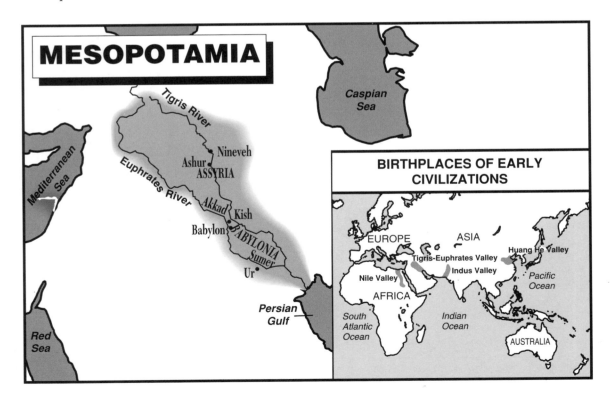

Mesopotamia was the first to appear, making this garden the "cradle of civilization," a name appropriate for the place where the first "infant" civilization grew.

The Ancient Near East is called the Middle East today. Its topography, or the lay of the land, has changed little over the thousands of years since people created cities along the banks of the Tigris and Euphrates Rivers. Bounded on the east by the Zagros Mountains, on the north by the Taurus Mountains, on the west by the Mediterranean Sea, and on the south by the Arabian Desert, a crescent-shaped arc of land follows the river valleys north, crosses over, and follows the Mediterranean coast south. This arc of land, called the Fertile Crescent, produces vegetation and provided a way of living for ancient people. The cradle began on the eastern side of the Fertile Crescent at its southern tip, the place later called Sumer. While Sumerian culture influenced the entire Ancient Near East, it most directly influenced the valleys of the two rivers. The achievements of the Sumerians influenced other cultures long after the empire of Sumer had ceased to exist.

A century and a half ago, archaeologists and scholars knew nothing about the Sumerians. They began excavating in Mesopotamia in the 1840s, but they were looking for Assyrian culture and Babylon, trying to discover evidence for history told in the Old Testament, the Hebrew Bible. Since no written history existed to tell about the first stages of life in Sumer, knowledge about the first civilization has depended on the work of archaeologists, who excavate mounds of dirt on the desert. Such digging has been going on for over a century by teams from many countries.

How Archaeologists Work

Archaeologists dig up the past and work with historians to draw conclusions from the remains. In early excavations, archaeologists merely hunted for objects for museums to display. Around 1900 German archaeologists developed a systematic method for excavating sites called tells. A tell is a mound that holds layers and layers of remains; ancient people repeatedly raised new buildings on the ruins of earlier buildings, gradually building up a mound. To excavate a tell, archaeologists mark off fifteen-meter squares, separated by one-meter spaces. Within a square, they dig carefully with small hand tools. They keep and label every object they find, even items that are small and broken. These objects, which may include pieces of written text as well as handmade goods of all kinds, human and animal bones, and natural substances that have been used by people, are known as artifacts. Archaeologists also study the walls that develop as the digging proceeds; these undisturbed spaces between the squares, called balks, show how many layers of culture occupied the site and when.

In less than a century of serious study, scholars have discovered that by 6000 B.C. Sumerians had already developed a complex society. Over time they developed agriculture and a system of irrigation, invented the wheel and made carts, created a religion and built grand temples for its priests and worshipers, invented a system of writing and numbers, and organized a way to govern the people, who lived in towns and cities. Sumerian achievements remained in place, even when other groups invaded and took over. By 300 B.C.,

Archaeologists work at a tell in Iraq. By sifting through the layers of remains in this tell, archaeologists will be able to piece together the history of early Mesopotamian civilizations.

however, this civilization had reached its peak, declined, and died; others had conquered it and imposed their ideas and ways of life.

How Historians Work

Scholars can now tell at least a partial story of the civilization that flowered in Mesopotamia thousands of years before the culture of the ancient Greeks and Romans. When historians relate sequences of events, they define terms, identify patterns in the events they narrate, and tell history's story according to a plan. The word *civilization* comes from the Latin word *civis,* or citizen. While historians differ somewhat in their use of the term, all defi-

nitions of civilization include the idea of people living in towns and cities and interacting socially in complex ways. Civilized people have achieved some control over nature and have developed laws, government, business, religion, art, and writing. These achievements they pass on to future generations. Sumerians began developing these elements eight thousand years ago.

Moreover, historians see different patterns in collections of historical events. While they are all curious about why some civilizations vanish while others continue, each one may interpret the causes and effects differently. The historian Carroll Quigley says that three conditions allow a civilization to rise, grow, and stay alive: first, people want to invent new ways of doing things; second, they begin to accumulate a surplus of wealth not needed for daily living; and third, they invest the surplus wealth in more new inventions. A civilization begins to decline and eventually dies when it ceases to acknowledge the need for inventions or fails to accumulate wealth for reinvestment in research and development.

According to Quigley, the pattern from the beginning to the end of a civilization can be traced in seven stages.

First, mixture. A civilization does not begin until two or more cultures mix, merge, and form a new culture.

Second, gestation. Civilizations go through a period of initial growth when people begin to invent, to accumulate wealth, and to make investments.

Third, expansion. Civilizations grow as standards of living rise, populations increase, borders expand, and knowledge accumulates.

Fourth, conflict. Civilizations experience conflict when expansion declines. Then class tensions increase, there are wars, and an atmosphere of pessimism prevails.

Fifth, universal empire. Civilizations develop a single government powerful enough to appear peaceful and prosperous, but the few in power squander wealth while the majority struggle to make a living.

Sixth, decay. Civilizations decay when the wealth is used up and economic depression sets in. Living standards and literacy decline, and conflicts within the society multiply.

Seventh, invasion. Civilizations grow too weak to defend themselves, making it possible for outsiders to invade and take over.

Quigley remarks that civilizations go through these stages at different rates. The first civilization completed the seven-stage cycle in a period of five or six thousand years.

By studying the Ancient Near East, we learn how a civilization arose out of the desert and was buried by the desert. We learn how the work of archaeologists and historians brought this impressive civilization out of the sand again and explained how it rose and fell. And we learn that these ancient peoples made contributions, directly and indirectly, to the lives of people living in the twentieth century.

1 Mixture: The First Farms, 6000–5000 B.C.

We cannot identify exactly which ancient tribes formed the mixture that developed the first civilization. Bits and pieces of information show that two or more groups of people settled in an area near the mouths of the Tigris and Euphrates Rivers somewhere between 8000 and 7000 B.C. and developed a way of life complex enough to be defined as a civilization. What happened there was indeed rare. In the last ten thousand years, only twenty-four civilizations have developed in the entire world, and only seven are still alive.

On the other hand, simple societies were common. People gathered into groups because they wanted to satisfy basic needs, such as security, wealth, power,

companionship, and understanding. The first societies roamed in small bands, gathering seeds and stalks and hunting wild herds. Their homes were caves, their clothes skins, and their tools stones. Excavations from the whole area of the Ancient Near East reveal evidence that many groups of people, once hunting and plant-gathering societies, settled into planting and herding societies. According to archaeologist Georges Roux, at some point

man ceases to be a wandering hunter depending for his living upon his luck and skill and becomes a farmer attached to the small piece of land from which he obtains a regular food supply.

Prehistoric men hunt a wild ox. Initially, humans were nomadic, moving to wherever animals were plentiful.

Farmers and Herders

In Sumer and the Sumerians, *historian Harriet Crawford comments on the mixture of settlers and nomads and the problems of obtaining reliable information.*

"Even though it is not possible to distinguish different physical types in early Mesopotamia, there was undoubtedly one very important dichotomy [set of opposing qualities] in the population, that between the settled villagers and the nomadic herders. The division between them was not always a clear-cut one. . . . Observations suggest that there is a natural tendency among pastoralists [herders] for the richest and poorest members of the group to drift into permanent settlement. The reasons for this are largely economic. The largest flocks suffer from the law of diminishing returns and profits and are better invested in something else, often property, while the poorest members of the group are often forced into towns to look for work. The steady increase in the number of Semitic personal names, often those of nomads, found in the archives of the third millennium towns [towns that existed between 3000 and 2000 B.C.], where the early names are predominantly Sumerian, suggests that just such a movement was taking place. . . .

Nomadic pastoralists are hard to identify in the archaeological record because of the sparseness of their material possessions and the perishable nature of many of their artifacts, rugs, leather bags and so on. This lack of an archaeological presence has led to their role in prehistoric times being underestimated until relatively recent times. It is probable that they had an important role to play in the diffusion of both raw materials and ideas."

Out of clay he builds himself a house. He invents new tools to perform new tasks. He secures in sheep and cattle a permanent and easily available source of milk, meat, wool and hide. At the same time his social tendencies develop, for the care and defense of the land call for close co-operation. Each family probably erects its own farm, cultivates its own field, grazes its own flock and makes its own tools; but several families are grouped together and form a hamlet [a small village], the embryo of a social organization.[1]

When two such hamlets or minisocieties border each other, their members interact. People borrow new ways from each other, and some marry members of the other group. Historian Carroll Quigley says: "Every civilization, indeed every society, begins with a mixture of two or more cultures. . . . But such casual cultural mixture is of little significance unless there comes into existence . . . a new culture, arising from the mixture but different from the constituent [separate] parts."[2] In Sumer, societies mixed, and a new culture arose. But who were these societies? And how did they get there?

Semites and Highland Garden People

By studying evidence from excavation sites, scholars think a society of Semitic (Arabic) people mixed with a society of Highland people who came from the foothills of the Zagros Mountains in the north. Historians are unable, however, to determine which group settled the area first. A group of southern Semites may have passed from a hunting society to a farming and herding society and settled first. Or perhaps Highland people moved south, and the Semitic hunters moved in later. Or during dry years, Semitic desert nomads (wanderers) may have moved out of the desert toward the rivers after the Highland farmers had become established. Whatever the order, people with many different characteristics came together. According to Quigley, the Semites, who were hunters and nomads, "tended to be warlike and patriarchal, and, in religion, emphasized the power of masculine sky gods, while the Highland dwellers tended to be more peaceful, more matriar-

chal, and had as their chief a goddess of fertility and sex who resided in the earth."[3]

The Invention of Agriculture

Of the two early groups, more is known about the Highland people than the Semites. The Highland people are credited with two of the major achievements of prehistoric times: They invented agriculture and began the practice of domesticating, or taming, animals. Soon after 10,000 B.C., people living on the slopes of the Taurus and Zagros Mountains settled into the first farming communities. Agriculture evolved slowly over centuries, but some person must have had the original idea. After gathering wild grains, someone must have thought along these lines: "If we save some of these seeds and plant them

Using only his hands for tools, an early human digs into the soil to plant seeds. Agriculture played a primary role in allowing humans to settle into permanent communities.

around our cave, we can stay in one place and avoid wandering in search of scattered patches of wild wheat and barley." Planting then required the use of tools—hoes—to till the soil and to make holes for seeds. Storage required bins and granaries.

Planting crops evolved hand in hand with the gradual domestication of certain animals. After a long hunting trip for meat and skins, one of the participants must have thought: "If we tame these wild goats and sheep and breed them so that they multiply into herds, which we will confine to our cave area, we can stay in one place and avoid long searches for game." Like planting crops, domesticating animals required additional new inventions, such as implements for feeding and herding. In these early farming villages, women took charge of planting, and men managed the animals.

Settling in one place required more complex ways of living. Excavations show that settlers made pressed-mud houses and invented more refined stone tools. Living in one location instead of wandering endlessly allowed people to spend more time making sharper knives and better pounding tools, to accumulate more possessions, and to store surpluses. From coils of clay, women made pots—large and small ones, tall and flat ones—to use for cooking and eating. Members of small families joined other family units and formed clans that required leaders and rules to accommodate new forms of social interaction. Invention of agriculture brought radical changes, but its inventors still lacked knowledge of nature and storms and seasons, and they had no idea what caused events they could observe.

Out of these early agricultural conditions evolved religious ideas. When the people observed that female animals and women produced young and that the earth produced crops, they assumed that there must be some connection. From these observations and thoughts developed a belief in an earth mother goddess, whom they associated with the power of human and animal fertility. The belief that the birth of young was connected with the growth of crops prevailed for thousands of years in the Ancient Near East. Because, like the earth, human mothers produced new life, women acquired high social and economic status.

Tigris and Euphrates River Valleys

Early farmers found that they could till the soil in one region for about seven or eight years before the soil wore out and crop yields diminished. Because they knew nothing about crop rotation or fertilizers, they abandoned the huts near worn-out fields and started new farms in other areas. For years, they followed this practice, moving their villages over the hills of the Highland Zone. Settling temporarily near a series of springs and streams in lower valleys, they worked their way southward. Eventually they reached the Tigris and Euphrates river valleys, which were rich with sediment left when the rivers overflowed their banks. Because this overflow occurred every year, farmers could plant crops on new sediment year after year without depleting the soil. Here the Highland people made permanent settlements.

Success in agriculture, however, depended on the rivers. The extent of the

Confusion in Religion

When the religions of the Semites and the Highland farmers mixed, gods changed in their importance. Such confusion is to be expected according to historian Carroll Quigley in The Evolution of Civilizations: An Introduction to Historical Analysis.

"When the neolithic peasant peoples [those who invented agriculture] developed civilizations in the [fertile] river valleys, males became more significant in their social, economic, and political life, and the sun became much more significant in their economic activities. In religion this served to reduce the earth goddess to a secondary role and make a male solar deity of primary significance. But this whole development was much confused by the persistent intrusion of Semite religious ideas in which the moon was male and of more importance. The rather chaotic ideas on these matters to be found in Mesopotamia in the historic period were thus a consequence of cultural mixture, and not a reflection of incapacity to think clearly."

annual flood on the plain depended on the amount of snow melting off the Taurus and Zagros Mountains and flowing into the upper Tigris and Euphrates Rivers. The rivers overflowed between April and June, too late to water winter crops and too early for summer crops, and yet no crops grew without the flood. The climate on the lower plain produced less than ten inches of rain in winter and almost none in summer, when temperatures soared above a hundred degrees. In years of scant snow and little melting, people had poor crops and famine; in years of heavy snow and high water, people lost their villages and all they owned. Archaeologist Georges Roux describes these conditions:

The rivers break through their embankment; the low land, as far as the eye can see, is submerged; the flimsy mud-houses and reed-huts are swept away; the crop is lost in a huge muddy lake, together with the cattle and the belongings of a large part of the population. . . . Thus Mesopotamia constantly hovers between a state of desert and gigantic swamp.[4]

A solution to the flood problem required control over nature, and the farmers developed an irrigation system. First, farmers and their children watered crops by carrying water from the river in clay vessels. Later, along the river's edge, they cut through the natural levees (ridges) and diverted the course of the water. They created dams to make pools and dipped water out of them with bailing buckets tied onto poles. Gradually, they made longer canals and dug them in courses that suited their plantings. To make and maintain an irrigation system, people gathered in large communities to centralize the work. Building canals and dikes required planning, new inventions, and different kinds of specialized knowledge, initiating division of labor, a key element in every civilization. Members of the merged groups had made a significant invention when they built an irrigation system.

Evidence of Mixture

Three kinds of evidence suggest that the savage and warlike Semite hunters or nomads from the south mixed with the peaceful Highland people from the north. First, the people developed a sexagesimal number system, a system based on 60. This system seems to have developed from a fusion of a decimal system (based on 10), a duodecimal system (based on 12), and perhaps a third system based on 20. This works out neatly because 60 can be divided into whole parts by 10, 12, and 20. Pottery decorated with the twelve signs of the zodiac has been found in Highland Zone sites, indicating that those people had the duodecimal system. And the decimal system is thought to have come from the Semitic peoples. The sexagesimal number system has given us a circle with 360 degrees, an hour with 60 minutes, and a year with 12 months.

Second, evidence from excavations shows that the inhabitants on the sediment-enriched plains kept sheep, goats, cattle, asses, fowl, and swine. Archaeological records indicate that the Highland Zone people had domesticated goats, sheep, and cattle. Semites in the south had grazed herds of asses. Fowl and swine were once tropical livestock. The co-existence of these species in pre-Sumer culture suggests that two or more societies had mixed their animals.

Third, changes in gods and changes in men's and women's roles also suggest that two or more societies mixed. The Highland Zone people had as their chief deity (god or goddess) an earth mother goddess, represented by a female figurine; if they regarded the sun as a god at all, it was male. On the other hand, Semites, who watched their herds day and night, used phases of the moon to keep track of time and considered the moon a male god; the sun, the moon's partner, was considered a

A figure of a fertility goddess found in the Jordan River valley dates back to 6000 B.C. By finding artifacts from different cultures in the same spot, archaeologists can trace the movement and merging of early societies.

goddess. Early Semitic cultures called the moon god Sin and the sun goddess Shapash. As agriculture developed and men took over the activities of planting, animal tending, and irrigating fields, the sun, now seen as important for crops, became a male god and the status of the earth mother goddess became less important. In other words, two systems of deities blended and emerged as a new system.

Determining which inventions occurred in the first period, the period of mixture, is an uncertain task because few records exist and because changes came gradually, but a few conclusions are possible. To make permanent settlements, some people built houses of sticks and woven reeds drawn together at the top and packed with clay. Others made *pisé*, houses built by a process of piling up mud. As time went on, people learned first to shape mud bricks with their hands and then to use molds to form mud bricks. Excavations show that some of the oldest houses had a lintel, a log placed above an opening to form a doorway. As agriculture developed, farmers invented implements to make their work easier. The most important invention was the plow. The first plow was probably a crooked tree branch used by two people, one pushing and one pulling. With it a farmer made furrows in which to lay rows of seeds, rather than digging separate holes. The plow made agriculture much more efficient later when people learned how to make copper plowshares and use the power of an ox in the pulling part of the job.

Another important invention was the wheel, thought by some to have been a modification of a potter's wheel. Because clay was abundant, these settlers used many pots, but fashioning pots from coils of clay took time. No one seems to know who invented the first potter's wheel to speed up the process. Apparently, however, it took only a few leaps of the imagination to turn two potter's wheels on their sides and put a stick between them to make an axle-wheel assembly for the first crude wagon, and then to add a second pair of wheels for a bigger vehicle. Since

Early people plant crops using crude plows and hoes. Such inventions showed an increased level of cultural sophistication.

Early potters fashion pots from coils of clay. Historians think perhaps the first wheel may have been a potter's wheel, used to produce pots.

people lived in villages and farmed the outlying fields, use of wagons to haul their implements and grain saved time and energy and, consequently, increased the crop yields.

Artifacts from Tells

Artifacts providing evidence for mud bricks, plows, wheels, and other inventions have been found at excavation sites. Since the first villages had no known names or exact dates, excavation sites and levels of digging often serve instead of dates. Artifacts from the northern farming communities correspond to artifacts from sites in

the south, suggesting that the farmers had moved south. In modern Iraq, for example, at Tell Hassuna, south of Mosul in the foothills of the northern Zagros Mountains near Nineveh, archaeologists found six layers of houses, each layer bigger and better built. Archaeologist Georges Roux describes them:

> Around a courtyard, six or seven rooms were arranged in two blocks, one block serving as living quarters, the other as kitchen and stores. The walls were made of adobe [lumps of clay pressed into bricks], the floors paved with a mixture of clay and straw. Grain was stored in huge bins of unbaked clay sunk in the ground up to

their mouth, and bread was baked in domed ovens. . . . Large jars kept inside the houses contained the bones of deceased children accompanied by tiny cups and pots for after-life refreshment.[5]

At Tell Halaf, west of Mosul, archaeologists found similar houses, though bigger and better built than those at Hassuna, and they also found other interesting artifacts. They found beehive-shaped *pisé* structures, built on circular stone foundations, buildings perhaps used as shrines or village meetinghouses. They found soapstone pendants with loops on the back and lines or crisscross patterns engraved on the front. The patterns were personal identification codes: They showed ownership when used to mark a lump of clay fastened to a jar or basket, and probably they were worn around the neck, as well. These soapstone pendants are the first examples of stamp-seals, a practical object that developed into an art form in the south. In addition, archaeologists found amulets (good-luck charms) shaped like a bull's head and clay figurines of a mother goddess. Similar items and practices appeared in southern excavation sites, suggesting that the farmers migrated south and continued to modify their customs in their new homes.

By 5000 B.C., the inhabitants of the fertile plain of the Tigris and Euphrates Rivers had become a new society developed from the mixture of two or more societies. They had invented an irrigation system and successful methods of farming, both of which contributed to a food supply sufficient to feed the population, with plenty to spare. Since their environment lacked stone, minerals, and wood, they used their surplus grain to trade with societies that had these resources. Consequently, trade routes had developed primarily toward the north and across to the Mediterranean Sea, but in other directions too. The first roads were nothing more than coarse tracks, but they allowed the new society to trade and grow. The Highland-Semitic people were on their way to becoming a civilization.

2 Gestation: The First Cities, 5000–4500 B.C.

Societies rise to civilization slowly at first, with little fanfare. Like a fetus in its mother's womb, a society in gestation begins and grows gradually.

After long periods of struggle—settling down and starting farms—the inhabitants on the Tigris-Euphrates plain could improve their lives. By 5000 B.C., the mixture of people had the start of an agricultural society dependent on an irrigation system. For the next five hundred years, the villagers ambitiously improved their farming system and developed a complex society. As far as anyone knows, they did not yet have a name. Some records indicate that the area was simply called "the Land."

Important new inventions improved irrigation and made farming productive. Building canals that extended farther from the river and brought water to locations convenient for watering crops required sophisticated engineering skills. Planners needed leveling instruments, measuring rods, and maps to design a system of dikes and reservoirs (places for storing water). They had to bring water to every field, but not so much that the canals overflowed. As farmers improved methods of training oxen to pull loads, they developed new implements for plowing, seeding, and harvesting. In addition, they invented ideas for better farming. For example, they found that by planting rows of palm trees, they could protect vegetable gardens from the hot sun and burning winds. This practice enabled them to grow chickpeas, lentils, vetches (herbs), onions, garlic, lettuce, turnips, watercress, leeks, mustard, and cucumbers.

The First Farmer's Almanac

The people of "the Land" produced the first farmer's manual a thousand years earlier than any other farmer's guidebook that has been found. Written by a Sumerian teacher over two thousand years after the gestation period, the manual contains refinements developed over time. The basic practices that continued throughout Sumerian history, however, had been formulated by farmers of an earlier age. A tablet with 109 lines, the first "farmer's almanac" begins with the words, "In days of yore a farmer gave (these) instructions to his son."[6] The annual agricultural cycle began with flooding the fields in May and June and ended with the care of harvested crops the following April and May. Among other particulars, the son was advised not to let water rise too high and to see that no oxen or "prowlers" trample the wet

The Farmer's Almanac

In History Begins at Sumer, *historian Samuel Noah Kramer quotes the first eighteen lines of the first farmer's handbook, as translated by himself and fellow cuneiformists Benno Landsherger and Thorkild Jacobsen. Kramer points out that the translation "will no doubt be considerably improved over the years as our knowledge of Sumerian language and culture grows."*

"In the days of yore a farmer gave (these) instructions to his son: When you are about to cultivate your field, take care to open the irrigation works (so that) their water does not rise too high in it (the field). When you have emptied it of water, watch the field's wet ground that it stays even; let no wandering ox trample it. Chase the prowlers and have it treated as settled land. Clear it with ten narrow axes (weighing no more than) ⅔ of a pound each. Its stubble (?) should be torn up by hand and tied in bundles; its narrow holes shall be gone over with a drag; and the four sides of the field shall be fenced about. While the field is burning (in the summer sun) let it be divided up into equal parts. Let your tools hum with activity (?). The yoke-bar should be made fast, your new whip should be fastened with nails, and the handle to which your old whip was fastened should be mended by the workers' children."

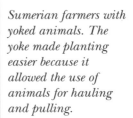

Sumerian farmers with yoked animals. The yoke made planting easier because it allowed the use of animals for hauling and pulling.

ground after the water had subsided. The ground needed to be broken twice with a mattock (digging tool) and once with a hoe; large clods had to be smashed with a hammer. It was desirable to have an extra ox on hand. In addition, the son was instructed to see that laborers did not shirk their work.

In this stone relief, a Mesopotamian woman spins wool using a spindle. Spinning and weaving were time consuming. A team of three women had to work for eight days to complete a piece of cloth large enough to make a garment.

The father also told his son to plow eight seeding furrows in every twenty-foot strip, and, in the words of the handbook, "keep an eye on the man who puts in the barley seed that he make the seed fall two fingers [deep] uniformly." When the seed "breaks through the ground," the son was to pray to Ninkilim, the goddess of field mice and vermin, to prevent these creatures from destroying the new shoots. The manual goes on to tell how many times to water, when to harvest the barley, and what tools and workers to employ for threshing. The almanac closes by saying that the rules come not from the father, but from the god Ninurta, the farmer son of Enlil, one of the principal deities.

Many generations of farmers benefited from such sound advice, and their communities prospered. As agriculture grew, so too did related industries that provided equipment for farmers and processed agricultural products. Consequently, the society needed artisans and people skilled in a variety of crafts. With growing herds of cattle, pigs, goats, and especially sheep, leather workers were kept busy making water containers, bags for carrying nonliquids, harnesses, shoes, and sandals. Sheep were sheared by plucking out small tufts of wool, which were spun into thread with a spindle and woven on a loom. It took a team of three women eight days to spin and weave a piece of cloth ten feet by thirteen feet.

The materials and goods had to be moved, giving rise to a transportation industry. Heavy loads were moved on a sledge, which was a box mounted on runners and pulled by a man or an ox. After the invention of the wheel, two- and four-wheeled wagons of various sizes became necessary. The river and canals also transported goods. Samuel Noah Kramer, an authority on Sumerian culture, explains:

> The common boat in use was the one known today in Iraq as the *guffa* and in ancient times as "the turnip"; it was made of reeds, covered with skin, and shaped like a basket. The sailboat, too, was probably known in ancient Sumer. . . . Oars and punting poles [long poles to push a boat forward] were in common use from earliest times. Along the river banks, however, the boats were often pulled by men or oxen.[7]

In this relief from Sumer dated from the third millennium B.C., men hunt in the marshes using a reed boat. These boats, still used today by the people of Iraq, allowed early peoples to transport goods along rivers and streams.

To this day, farmers work at the mercy of nature, but the earliest farmers also lacked all scientific knowledge to help them reduce their risks. The need to determine when the flood would arrive led to the first astronomical studies. Historian Carroll Quigley describes the farmers' plight:

> It takes an imaginative effort on our part to picture the minds of these early peasants who were ignorant of what we take to be self-evident. They had no calendars or other methods for keeping track of time; in fact they hardly recognized the existence of time as we know it. They knew nothing of the year or of the movements of the earth that determine it; they had no knowledge of the causes of the flood and, at the beginning, may not even have recognized that it was periodic. Above all, they could not have imagined any connection between the movements of the sun and the arrival of the flood.[8]

Someone must have noted that the sun rises at different points on the horizon and moves higher in the sky and then returns. Someone must have invented a way to mark the point of each day's sunrise and perhaps, the angle of the sun in relation to the earth. With that information, a person could eventually figure out a solar year. In time someone must have noticed that the flood always came when the sun had reached a certain point in the sky, knowledge that increased the farmers' ability to plan and, consequently, gave them more control over nature and their lives.

A Religion with Many Gods

The limited scientific knowledge of the time was insufficient to give peace of mind to the people who lived in such a precarious environment. Thus, there evolved a philosophical system based on many gods to explain the workings of the universe. Today we call such a system of thought a religion, but the Sumerians of seven thousand years ago had no comparable term. Since what we know about early religions is based on information scholars have derived from documents written much later, we can only guess how much of the Sumerian religious system had developed by 4500 B.C. Of the earliest gods, the four most important were An, the heaven or sky god; Enlil, the air god; Enki, the water god; and Ninhursag, the great mother goddess. Though the gods remain the same, names vary in different places and at different times. The gods met as an assembly, with Enlil, the father of the gods, as ruler. At one point, in addition to the four most important gods, there were seven gods who decreed the fate of the world, fifty great gods, and the tutelary gods—the deities that individuals and families worshiped as their personal guardians. Not all gods had equal rank; for example, the pickax god was less important than the sun god, the god of ditches and dikes less important than the god of the whole world.

The people thought their gods had human qualities, or personhood. They reasoned about the gods from their own lives. Their farms and cities crumbled if neglected. Therefore, since the universe is a larger collection of cities and representatives of nature, it too must be tended and cared for, and that is what gods do. Since the universe is larger and more complex than its parts, the gods must be stronger and more powerful than people. And they must be immortal, since the universe would not run properly if the gods died and left it unattended. The people thought their gods lived on a mountain where the sun rose and that they behaved much as humans behave—planning, working, eating and drinking, marrying and raising families, and experiencing the same emotions and weaknesses.

Two religious beliefs seem to have existed from the beginning of the culture. One developed around the fertility cult. The Highland people had regarded women as productive, both of crops and of children, and they symbolized their reverence for women in the earth mother goddess, which they represented as a female figurine, usually pregnant and having excessively large breasts. When the societies mixed, the resulting culture gave more importance to men and eventually recognized the male role in reproduction. The male characteristic of virility, symbolized by the bull, became as important as the female's fertility. The earth mother now had a lover who was associated with the sun. As the sun came and went, so too did crops grow and die, and the male sun god was depicted in the people's myths as a god that died and was resurrected every year. In time the female became associated with the moon and its monthly cycle. Symbols evolved, as did rituals and ceremonies, as if somehow human activity enhanced the gods' fertility and fruitfulness, and, subsequently, people's own capacity to be productive.

The second religious belief developed around the idea of providing for the gods.

The people saw the gods as having power to control human life. They also believed the gods had human needs and required to be fed. By thought processes we can only guess at, they evolved the idea that it was important to feed the gods generously because the gods would be more apt to grant favors and good harvests to the ones who fed them. Likewise, people could offer gifts to avoid trouble and disfavor from the gods. From this idea developed the practice of giving the gods part of the harvest and some of their livestock. To help ensure that the gods knew who had made what offering, ceremonies and rituals were developed to accompany the delivery of the worshipers' gifts.

Development of a Priesthood

Several elements in the new culture came together in the rise of a priesthood. One element was administrative. As irrigation developed, someone in town took charge of planning and commanding the workforce that built and maintained the system. Another element was economic. Those knowledgeable in astronomy could best predict when the flood would come; they gained wealth and power by charging a certain amount of grain for their technical knowledge. The other elements were religious. In addition to specialists able to formulate ceremonies and rituals, people needed a place to perform the rites and to store surplus gifts of grain. The building that met these needs was the forerunner of the temple, and the manager of the various activities, the priest, was called an *en*. As the population grew and ceremonies became more elaborate, the priesthood also grew into a large group with specialized jobs. As these management tasks fell to the priests, the priesthood gained more and more power in the community. Men and women alike served as priests.

Five Important Excavation Sites

Five excavation sites have provided artifacts from the gestation period. From the findings at digging sites, archaeologists and historians piece together the history of a place. The main digging site in Mesopotamia was at Ur, where Sir Leonard Woolley excavated down to original soil through many layers of development. Eridu, sixteen miles southwest of Ur, was one of the oldest cities in the area.

This necklace was found at Ur during an excavation. Archaeological digs in the area revealed many clues to several important ancient cities.

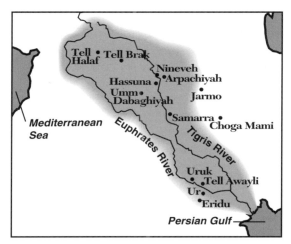

Some of the prehistoric sites from which early farmers may have migrated to cities such as Ur and Eridu.

from the early Highland people. They found axes, clay nails, baked clay sickles for cutting grain, and a clay model of a boat. Outside the city wall, in a cemetery with a thousand graves, they found bodies buried in rectangular shafts lined with mud brick. In one a dog had been buried with its master. Cylinder-seals found at the Eridu site depict the architecture of reed-built houses, which look like those of the so-called Marsh Arabs of Iraq, who occupy the area today. The cylinder-seal, a short clay tube with a design around the outside, replaced the stamp-seal to show ownership; an owner rolled the cylinder into soft clay and left his design to mark his possessions.

Before archaeologists unearthed it, Ubaid, which turned out to be an aban-

Ubaid, four miles northwest of Ur, represents the period of the earliest artifacts. Uruk, farther northwest of Ur, represents the period just later than Ubaid. Both the Ubaid and Uruk periods occurred before the Great Flood, tentatively dated at 2800 B.C. Jemdat Nasr, a city much farther north from Ur, brought inventions to Uruk when its people occupied it. Jemdat Nasr represents the first period after the flood. What have archaeologists found at each of these sites?

Eridu, thought later Sumerian writers, was the oldest city in the world. Because Enki, the water god, was said to have his earthly residence there, Eridu was one of the most sacred cities. Archaeologists found ruins of seventeen temples built one on top of the other, the lowest three from the gestation period. Built of mud bricks, each bearing a thumbprint, these one-room temples served to house an altar, or offering table. Archaeologists also found many clay objects. Among them were terra-cotta (brownish orange clay) figurines of the mother goddess, probably

A Babylonian cylinder-seal shows the early sun and moon gods. Such seals, which replaced the earlier stamp-seals, were used in ancient Mesopotamia to mark a person's possessions.

doned city as old as Eridu, was nothing but an unidentified six-foot-high mound rising above the plain. Besides clay objects like the ones dug up at Eridu, archaeologists found thread spun from wool, cow dung mixed into the mud plaster, and a clay figurine of a pig, indication that the inhabitants had kept a variety of domestic animals. Archaeologists found temples built of mud bricks set in clay mortar—temples like the ones found at Eridu, but bigger. Besides an altar, the Ubaid temples had a low platform, probably the base for a statue of a god. The distinguishing feature of the Ubaid dig was its painted pottery, which shows the superior artistry of the earliest settlers. These unknown artisans probably "brought with them a ceramic style which had been developed in their original home."[9] The pots, which seem to have been made on a primitive pottery wheel, were decorated with triangles, stripes, and crosshatched bands. The colors ranged from buff (cream) to green with dark decorations only on part of each pot.

Uruk, the city called Erech in the Old Testament and Warka today, reveals more rapid development of this southern culture. The city was dedicated to two deities—An, the sky god, and Inanna, the goddess of love—and the temples were found in pairs. At the lowest level, the oldest, a temple dedicated to Inanna, had decorated walls; it measured 260 feet by 100 feet. At the entrance stood eight brick columns, each 8 feet in diameter. In another part of the city, a more modest temple honored the god An.

By this stage, cylinder-seals had completely replaced stamp-seals, and the carved specimens found at Uruk are "little masterpieces," according to archaeologist Georges Roux. Some designs symbolize the two deities; some feature an eagle, a snake, or a temple. Others have a bearded king attended by a priest, and others show flocks and herds defended by a bull-man. Toward the end of the Uruk period, writing appeared for the first time in history. The first "scripts" were tablets on which pictographic designs had been pressed into soft clay with a wedge-shaped reed. The tablets had pictographs for tools, implements, and vehicles, such as an ax, a plow, and a sledge. Cuneiform writing later developed out of pictographic writing.

Like the other ancient cities, Ur had layer upon layer of artifacts. After working through many layers, however, archae-

A cylinder-seal depicts men and bearded, upright animals. Unfortunately, archaeologists are not able to completely decipher the meaning of these depictions. The seals, however, remain wonderful examples of early artistic achievement.

ologist Leonard Woolley came to an eleven-foot layer of clean silt that contained no remains. Below the silt, he found three levels that had been occupied and finally a belt of mud, which represented the bottom of Mesopotamia. Woolley realized that the clean-silt layer was clay deposited by a major flood. He calculated that the water carrying that much silt must have been twenty-five feet deep and must have covered an area three hundred miles long and a hundred miles wide. Woolley says:

> We have proved that there really was a flood. . . . It was a vast flood . . . which drowned the whole of the habitable land between the mountains and the desert; for the people who lived there that was all the world. The great bulk of those people must have perished, and it was but a scanty and dispirited remnant that from the city walls watched the waters recede at last. No wonder that they saw in this disaster the gods' punishment of a sinful generation.[10]

Woolley identified this disaster as the biblical flood of Noah, and dated it later than the gestation period.

Jemdat Nasr, a city younger than Ur and farther north, is important because its artifacts also appear in Uruk. Jemdat Nasr had occupied Uruk for a time. The earliest written tablets came from Uruk, but the earliest tablets written in Sumerian came from Jemdat Nasr. During the occupation of Uruk, most customs and art remained the same, except for one thing; sculpture appeared for the first time. Excavators found a life-size mask of a woman made of marble. The eyes are missing, but

While excavating Ur, archaeologist Leonard Woolley found evidence that a devastating flood had left most of early Mesopotamian civilization under water. Woolley believed that this was historical proof of the biblical account of the great flood in the time of Noah.

the face is modeled to look realistic and sensitive. Most sculpture of the period, depicting animals and heroes, was carved in relief (figures projecting from a flat background).

The advances represented by artifacts found at Ubaid, Uruk, and Jemdat Nasr indicate that a new culture had indeed evolved out of a mixture, with abundant new inventions, grand architecture, and fine art. It was a culture about to become Sumerian civilization.

Chapter

3 Expansion: Life and Growth in the City-States, 4500–2500 B.C.

After slow growth, a society acquires many inventions and accumulates a supply of surplus goods. Then conditions are ripe for rapid expansion in many directions, and the society becomes a civilization. At this point in the history of the Tigris-Euphrates valley, the population increased, and people started new towns and cities. The people made additional inventions and improved old ones, production of crops increased, and the rising economy brought higher living standards to more people. Surpluses allowed for further trade. As the culture became more complex, knowledge increased, and the people invented writing, a way to preserve knowledge and to pass it on to the next generations. No single element caused the rapid expansion; rather, the combination of interrelated elements fueled growth to a level worthy to call this culture a civilization—the Sumerian civilization.

When the ruler of one city became politically strong enough to rule over the entire region, the area became known as Sumer. The word *Sumer* came from "Shinar," an older name for the plain. Sumer covered about ten thousand square miles, almost the size of the country of Belgium, extending from what is Baghdad today south to the marshes bordering the Persian Gulf. It grew into a country of thirteen cities, with Eridu, Uruk, Nippur, Lagash, Larsa, Kish, and Ur as the more important ones. Two cities north of this area, Mari on the Euphrates and Assur on the Tigris, also developed rapidly and came under Sumerian cultural influence. The size of Sumerian cities is uncertain, but scholars have tried to make estimates. Roux reports that Lagash had a population of 30,000–35,000; Kramer reports 100,000 for the city. Woolley estimates that Ur grew to a population of 360,000; Kramer thinks 200,000 is a closer estimate.

The Development of City-States

The cities grew into city-states, political-religious units consisting of a city itself, its suburbs, the outlying towns and villages, plus the land that made up its gardens, orchards, palm groves, and grainfields. The uncultivated areas between city-states served as pastureland and their ownership often was disputed among people from neighboring towns. The belief that gods controlled everything still prevailed. Since the city-states were thought to belong to the gods, strong central governments failed to develop. The temple became the center of activities, and the city-state came under the protection of the particular god who was thought to own the city. For example, Lagash belonged to Ningirsu, son of Enlil, and Ur belonged to Nanna, the moon god.

An adminstrator, called an *ensi*, governed the city-state and led the people from his offices in the temple. The temple administration collected the people's gifts, called "tributes"; stored grain in case of famine; traded surplus grain for imported metal, wood, and stone; built temples and fortifications; and directed canal projects. In addition, the temple employed scribes to record transactions of the institution's growing activities. The administration distributed the cultivated land surrounding the city to suit the temple system. One part was worked by the whole community for the sole benefit of the temple. Temple workers tilled another part for their own support, since salaries had yet to be invented. The remainder was plow land, acres rented to tenants who paid an eighth of the harvest as rent. Until the development of strong central governments with kings, the city-states functioned independently.

Gradually, as temples amassed wealth, rulers became kings, and city-states competed to control the entire region. During this time, societies began to produce documents called King Lists. The Sumerian King List, for example, gives the names of kings, the city-states they ruled, and dates for their reigns. The dates are not reasonable, however: The list identifies eight kings before the Flood reigning for a quarter-million years, for an average reign of more than thirty thousand years. After the Flood, supposedly, two dynasties ruled for twenty-five thousand years. (A dynasty is a series of rulers from the same family, or their appointed successors.)

Eventually, archaeologists discovered a tablet that provided a useful key to the King List. Even though for some reigns the dates given are pure fancy, the list is significant because it verifies names of Sumerian cities and their kings. The list shows, for example, that Gilgamesh of Erech, Agga of Kish, and Mesannepadda of Ur all reigned at the same time before the Flood, in the so-called First Dynasty; that the king of Kish was the most powerful king after the Flood; and that Urukagina of Lagash was the first pacifist—a king known not for war, but for social and ethical reforms.

Based on the belief that the gods had created everything, Sumerians believed that kingship descended from heaven before the Flood and again in Kish after the Flood. The kingship meant that each city god chose a king to be his earthly representative—to administer the god's property, to govern on the god's behalf, to build the god's temples, and to restore

Sumerian King Lists

The King Lists identify names of Sumerian kings and their cities. In the Appendixes to The Sumerians: Their History, Culture, and Character, *Professor Samuel Noah Kramer includes a translation of the Sumerian King List, portions of which are quoted here.*

"After kingship had descended from heaven, Eridu became (the seat) of kingship. In Eridu Alulim reigned 28,800 years as king; Alalgar reigned 36,000 years—two kings reigned 64,800 years. Eridu was abandoned, (and) its kingship was carried off to Badtibira. . . .

In Sippar, Enmeduranna reigned 21,000 years as king—one king reigned 21,000 years. Sippar was abandoned (and) its kingship was carried off to Shuruppak. . . .

The Flood then swept over (the land). After the Flood had swept over (the land) and kingship had descended from heaven (a second time), Kish became (the seat) of kingship. In Kish, Gaur reigned 1,200 years as king; Gulla-Nidaba-annapad reigned 960 years; Palakinatim reigned 900 years. . . .

In Ur, Mesannepadda reigned 80 years as king; Meskiagnunna, the son of Mesannepadda reigned 36 years as king; Elulu reigned 25 years; Balulu reigned 36 years. (Total) four kings reigned 177 years. Ur was defeated (in battle), (and) its kingship was carried off to Awan."

---

them when they were destroyed by an enemy. The distinction between the king and the god, however, is not immediately obvious to readers thousands of years later. Archaeologist Georges Roux offers this clarification:

There is also no doubt that the city chief [king] played a leading role in the New Year Festival and, on many occasions, acted as the male god in the Sacred Marriage ceremony. Indeed, there is reason to believe that, early in the third millennium [3000–2000 B.C.], during the "heroic age" of En-

merkar, Lugalbanda and Gilgamesh, certain Sumerian royal couples were considered as "living gods" or, more correctly, as human duplicates of the gods representing on earth the divine couple to which the city-state belonged.[11]

What is clear, however, is that the inhabitants of Sumer built grand buildings to honor their kings and their gods and the city-states accumulated massive wealth.

As the city-states grew and the kingship evolved, economic classes developed. Records show that the temples sold fields, houses, and movable items to individuals; even kings had to pay for property they took. In time, some families acquired large estates and became the nobility. Commoners too could buy their own plots of land and own houses and cattle. Eventually the population sorted into four classes: nobles, commoners, clients, and slaves. Clients owned nothing; they worked on the nobility's estates in return for their keep. Slaves were prisoners of war, former freemen being punished for offenses, and children whose parents had sold them to settle debts. The idea of slaves as property was universally recognized, and slaves could be branded and flogged for attempting to escape. Most owners, though, found that slaves who were healthy and happy made better workers. Slaves were not without rights in any event; they could engage in business, borrow money, and buy their own freedom. If a slave married a free person, any children the couple had were considered to be free. At one time the average price for a male slave was slightly less than the price of an ass.

Sumerian Family Life

Sumerians were an ambitious people concerned with family life and ethical values. Sumerian authority Samuel Noah Kramer says:

> The Sumerians prized highly wealth and possessions, rich harvests, well-stocked granaries, folds and stalls filled with cattle large and small, successful hunting on the plain and good fishing in the sea. The kings constantly boast in their hymns of bringing prosperity and well-being to the land and its people. . . . In the lamentations, the poets constantly and in no uncertain terms bemoan the loss of material possessions.[12]

For those who failed to work and succeed, Sumerians had many terms: among them are words that have been translated as "dolt," "numbskull," "pest," "bungler," and "windbag."

The family was the basic unit of society, through which the values of work and

Much as modern people do, Sumerians valued family and financial success and worked hard to increase both. In these scenes from about 3000 B.C., a team of slaves builds a brick wall (left), and three Sumerian men work in a dairy (right).

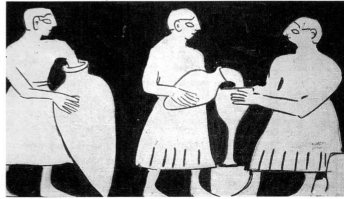

success were passed along. Even though parents arranged marriages, families created close relationships of respect and love. A woman had legal rights to own property and engage in business. A man had a right to divorce a wife on minor grounds or marry a second wife if his first wife had no children. Children seemed to have no rights; parents had absolute authority over them and could disinherit disobedient children or sell them into slavery, although these drastic measures were seldom invoked. Many couples adopted children and cared well for them, and society in general treated widows, orphans, and the poor with compassion.

City-states had laws to protect freedom and justice and to punish wrongdoers. A document from the city of Lagash shows that leaders, to raise money for their armies, had abused their power. They had seized animals, cheated on tributes, and charged excessive fees for divorces, sheep shearing, and burial taxes. The reform laws that tried to eliminate those abuses had a word for freedom, *amargi*, the first appearance in recorded history of a word representing this concept. Records show evidence of lawsuits, investigations, court cases, and verdicts that resulted in the awarding of damage payments to victims. Laws forbade the rich to force poor people to sell their donkeys and required that temple property be returned. Other laws granted food rations to craftsmen, blind laborers, temple singers, and artisans. One law said that if a woman said bad words to a man, her words had to be inscribed on a burned brick before her teeth were crushed. The law suggests that the process of inscribing her words on burned brick prevented the chance that a woman would be falsely punished. Further, the process

required time that allowed for tempers to cool and, perhaps, accusations to be dropped. Another said that a man who cut off another man's nose had to pay a fine in silver. The records show that such laws were a common custom before 2500 B.C.

Investment in Inventions

Much of the rapid expansion in Sumer occurred because wealth was invested to create new inventions and improve old ones. Historian Carroll Quigley says, "In this period some of the most significant advances in human history were either made or adapted to large-scale use."[13] Many inventions had been introduced years before. One of them, animal husbandry, continued to grow. Farmers increased their herds, commonly used donkeys for transportation, and later domesticated the horse; they created two hundred words for "sheep," the most common animal, and bred mountain sheep and goats, whose hair they used for carpets. Another early invention, metalwork, first developed in the Highland Zone. Since Sumer had no natural resources for metalwork, the *en* used surplus grain to trade for metals, a form of commerce made possible by the sailboat. With the invention of the sailboat, probably before 3000 B.C. on the Persian Gulf, Sumerians were able to obtain copper, gold, silver, and tin to invent jewelry, better plows, spears, helmets, and shields for war. Military leaders also devised new tactics of warfare, such as marching soldiers in rows.

Historians do not know the origin of the wheel, which appeared in Mesopotamia before 4000 B.C. Some thought the

Sumerians were especially good at using their wealth to produce inventions that improved their lives. (Left) A mold for casting gold jewelry dates from about 3000 B.C. (Below) A standard dating from 2500 B.C. shows helmeted lancers, chariots, horses, and weapons, suggesting that military preparation was important to these ancients.

now-familiar item appeared when someone turned a potter's wheel on its side. Others thought the first wheel was a slab of tree trunk, but this theory ignores the absence from the area of large trees. Another historian noted that the sun was painted on pottery in a spoked-wheel image. Thus, the wheel may have been invented when someone realized that the pottery sun disk would roll. Whatever the origin, Sumerians adapted the wheel for their flat land, to use on ceremonial carts, everyday wagons, and war vehicles.

Based on their sexagesimal number system, Sumerians made new mathematical inventions. They derived formulas to compute the area of a triangle and a trapezoid, and they devised the earliest known way to measure the volume for a cube. They had no zero and wrote a fraction like "¾" as "¼ plus ½," but they needed few fractions for a system based on 60, which is divisible by 1, 2, 3, 4, 5, 6, 10, 15, 20, 30, and itself. Sumerians also improved the management system for temples; documents show that they extended the areas handled by the priesthood to include the practice of international law and the development of methods for settling disputes by negotiation, rather than by war. And they invented beer, which was popular for medicinal purposes as well as for regular drinking. A special goddess took charge of beer preparation, Ninkasi, whose name means "the lady who fills the mouth."[14]

Sumerians improved inventions they had already made in the construction industry. Since the area has no stone and no large trees, finding materials presented a problem. There was mud, however, lots of it, and the people developed it in several stages, from *pisé* to burned bricks. First came adobe bricks formed by hand and then mud bricks made in a mold. Plano-convex bricks, rounded on one face and laid in alternating rows to give a herringbone look, constituted a more refined invention. Finally they made bricks of clay mixed with ground straw and fired in a kiln. From the invention of bricks came the invention of the arch, an alternative to the lintel. The Highland Zone people, as well as many cultures around the world, used the lintel, but only Sumerians had the arch. Historian Carroll Quigley called it "a very difficult invention, made only once in human history."[15] Mesopotamians had invented the arch by the fourth millennium B.C., probably by noticing that a cross-section of a dome had properties that would make an arch.

Temple Building

Sumerians used their finest architectural skills to build temples and, later, palaces. They first raised the temples above the ground on platforms; as their skills advanced, they built higher platforms. The earliest temples from the Ubaid period at Eridu consisted of a simple rectangular room flanked on both sides by smaller rooms, built on a low platform. The mosaic temple from the early Uruk period had the same floor plan, but was larger and had walls "decorated with stone cones of different colours, black, red and white arranged in geometric patterns." A temple from the late Uruk stage had a T-shaped floor plan, a higher platform, a "double row of eight free-standing columns, decorated with cone mosaic in red, black and white. The cones were of clay with painted heads to give the same effect as the differently coloured stones used in the [m]osaic temple."[16] Builders made bigger temples on higher platforms until they built the ziggurat, the grandest religious architecture of the civilization.

A ziggurat, from a word that means "to build high," is a temple tower, and every city had one dedicated to its patron deity. A ziggurat usually had at least three flat-topped stories, each one smaller than the one below it. On top was the god's shrine, which people could reach by climbing flights of stairs that ran around the outside of the structure. Two stories of the Third Dynasty ziggurat at Ur remain. Standing on a large terrace in the heart of the city, its base measures 200 feet by 150 feet, and the two stories reach 60 feet up. Its mud-brick construction had an 8-foot outer layer of baked bricks set in bitumen (a petroleum substance like tar). This huge ziggurat appeared lightweight and graceful because it was perfectly proportioned and its walls had slightly curved lines, a trick historians once thought had been devised by the Greeks two thousand years later. The ziggurat stood in a walled area that took up the northern half of Ur. It cast its shadow over a courtyard and the king's palace and reflected its image in the Euphrates River.

The Ziggurat

Sumerian city-states proudly displayed their ziggurats. In Sumer and the Sumerians, *historian Harriet Crawford discusses the importance of these structures.*

"The best known of the Sumerian religious monuments must be the great ziggurats or staged towers, which dominated the major cities. It seems that the ziggurat developed as a logical extension of the long-established tradition of raising temples on platforms or terraces above the surrounding buildings. This tradition can be traced back to the Ubaid period. The platforms, and later the ziggurats, both seem to have served the same purpose, to raise the home of the god even closer to the heavens. Scholars have debated for many years the purpose of these constructions. Their proposals cover a wide range of possibilities, from the suggestion that the ziggurat reflects a folk memory of the mountainous country from which the Sumerians may, or may not, have originated, to the theory that it was a giant sacrificial altar. The names of the ziggurats certainly include the word mountain in many cases, but this may be no more than a reference to their size and shape. High places are often regarded as holy places. Moses went up onto the mountain to receive the Ten Commandments and the Lord of the Old Testament often refers to his Holy Mountain."

An artist's conception of a Sumerian ziggurat from about 3000 B.C. The shrine of the patron deity was at the top of each multilayered temple.

This gold vessel (left) and these golden daggers (right) were found in Sumerian tombs. Because of objects found in such tombs, archaeologists think that the Sumerians believed in an afterlife.

Evidence from Tombs

Leonard Woolley's extensive excavations of burial sites at Ur, Sumer's leading city, reveal the customs and wealth of people in ancient times. The British archaeologist found commoners' graves and royal tombs. The dead who were not royalty were laid on their sides and wrapped in mattings or in coffins. Buried with them were beads, earrings, knives, cylinder-seals, and vessels to hold food and drink, but there were no god images. The objects seem to indicate that the families expected the dead to go to an afterlife. In the grave of an important man named Mes-kalam-dug, Woolley found spears of copper and gold, gold daggers, copper jugs, a silver belt, hundreds of gold beads, a gold bowl, and a beautiful gold wig hel-

met. In the tomb with him were a crowd of skeletons that had been wearing gold when they were buried, evidence that attendants died with the king. A line from a hero story of the time says that some of a hero's "retainers" accompany him in death. The objects in this grave, probably belonging to a rich commander or lugal (king), reveal the fine quality of the Sumerian metalworkers' art.

The royal tombs had many large rooms. Queen Shub-ad's tomb was built above King A-bar-gi's. Untouched by looters, the queen's chamber had skeletons of two companions, jewelry, and an elaborate headdress of gold and semiprecious stones. Around her were a gold container for her tweezers, silver and gold vessels, a harp decorated with a cow's head, a gaming table, and over two hundred other valuable objects. Her clothes had been packed in a chest sunk into the floor. The king had his own burial chamber and other rooms for members of his court. Woolley found gold daggers, tools, and a cylinder-seal buried with the king, as well as the remains of fifty-nine bodies, including six soldiers who had led the funeral procession, two chariots drawn by six oxen, nineteen court ladies in gold head-dresses, and four musicians. Near the musicians there was a little cup, placed in a way indicating that there had been a ceremony before the attendants and servants took poison. One anthropologist speculates that a twenty-five-inch silver boat found there was probably meant to carry the dead to the other world. The royal tombs reveal the amount of wealth kings accumulated. The elaborate burials also suggest that the rich used wealth for luxuries and not for investment in more inventions, a sign that the civilization had begun to decline.

Cuneiform Writing

In tells throughout Mesopotamia, archaeologists have found thousands of clay tablets inscribed with cuneiform characters. In this form of writing, which was invented in Sumer and evolved from pictographs, wedge-shaped marks were made with a sharp reed. Cuneiform writing is based on the following idea:

A cuneiform tablet from Lagash that dates from 3000 B.C. The development of cuneiform writing inspired a need for schools to train scribes who would be able to use the written language.

one object or idea=one sound=one
sign in cuneiform

Once modern scholars had deciphered the system, they were able to read the thousands of tablets found in the tells.

The earliest cuneiform tablets are lists of economic transactions made in temples. Later, scribes made lists of gods, tools and implements, birds and animals, and ideas. Many tablets record the literature. As early as the third millennium B.C., scribes had set up schools to teach cuneiform. Attended mostly by children from wealthy families, the *edubba*, the "tablet house," taught botany, zoology, mineralogy, mathematics, and grammar. The oldest known dictionaries were found in the *edubbas*. Historian Samuel Noah Kramer explains the importance of cuneiform and the schools that taught students to write it:

> From the point of view of the history of civilization, Sumer's supreme achievements were the development of the cuneiform system of writing and the formal system of education which was its direct outgrowth. It is no exaggeration to say that had it not been for the inventiveness and perseverance of the anonymous, practically oriented Sumerian pundits and teachers who lived in the early third millennium B.C., it is hardly likely that the intellectual and scientific achievements of modern days would have been possible; it is from Sumer that writing and learning spread the world over. To be sure, the inventors of the earliest Sumerian signs, the pictographs, could hardly have anticipated the system of schooling as it developed in later days.[17]

Sumerians invented practical objects, initiated efficient methods for government and industry, art and literature, and made other useful intellectual advancements.

4 Expansion: Religion and Art of Sumerian Dynasties, 4500–2500 B.C.

In a period of expansion, a civilization develops not only politically and economically, but also intellectually and artistically. In Sumer, the period of expansion began with the Early Dynastic period, when independent city-states came under the rule of one king, and extended through the Third Dynasty of Ur. A dynastic succession of kings usually passes from father to son, but that order was only sometimes followed in Sumer. Between the Early Dynasties and the Third Dynasty, a Semite, an outsider, ruled, but little changed because the Semite king adopted all the Sumerian customs and ideas. The period of the dynasties produced more refined religious thought and significant pieces of art and literature.

The concept of dynasties had its roots in the very first superheroes, and the concept of superheroes evolved from early merging of the roles of the city god and the city king. Both notions represent a gradual change from rule by gods to rule by humans. Superheroes, characters like Beowulf and Odysseus, were historical persons whose human qualities and accomplishments became exaggerated in the retelling of their stories.

The best known Sumerian superhero is Gilgamesh, who is also significant historically. His history is told in a cuneiform tablet called "Gilgamesh and Agga." Gilgamesh, who ruled Erech after the Flood, was gaining power. Kish's king Agga, worried that the ambitions of Gilgamesh might pose a threat to Kish, demanded that Erech submit to Kish or suffer consequences. Gilgamesh called a meeting of both parts of the governing assembly of his city. The members wanted to submit to Agga's ultimatum, but Gilgamesh, unsatisfied with the decision, called another meeting. This time the body voted to fight. When Agga and his men arrived to besiege Erech, Gilgamesh's warriors met the aggressors outside the city wall. When Agga saw that Gilgamesh had come out to fight, he abandoned the siege. Gilgamesh thanked him for his change of heart. The people of Erech praised Gilgamesh for saving their city, and an epic story grew around the king's bravery and his exploits. The historical story is important because it shows that a bicameral (two-part) governing body existed over five thousand years ago, the world's first political body.

The story also suggests how the dynasties developed. The king of a city-state amassed soldiers and wealth until he thought himself powerful enough to defeat other rulers. His army first attacked a neighboring city-state; if successful, he attacked others until he controlled the whole area. The King List shows how many times these struggles for power occurred. Each time, the victors burned and destroyed cities, especially the temples

Gilgamesh was a Sumerian king whose accomplishments were immortalized in the first great epic poem.

and palaces. Usually after destruction the victor rebuilt, or the city gained power again at a later date and the new leaders rebuilt. This obviously costly and wasteful practice accounts for the many layers of debris in Mesopotamian archaeological sites.

New Religious Beliefs

As the temples became more grand and rituals more elaborate, so too did religious beliefs become more complex. An upper class had developed—people with enough wealth to allow for leisure time to plan celebrations and to think about religious questions. The New Year festival, called *zagmuk*, was a celebration that took place every spring: "It is now generally admitted that each city-state ensured the fertility of its own fields and the fecundity [productivity] of its own people and cattle by means of a Sacred Marriage between its patron-god and one of its goddesses."[18] Archaeologist Georges Roux tells how the ceremony became more elaborate and acquired broader meaning:

> For eleven days the thoughts of the entire population were focused on the ceremonies which took place in the capital city, because they offered an answer to the fears and hopes of every Mesopotamian. It was felt that mankind shared in the great renewal undergone by nature, that the past was abolished, that the cosmos momentarily reverted to chaos [total disorganization], that the fate of the country depended upon the judgment pronounced by the gods. Nothing short of

a complex ritual loaded with magical virtues could solve the unavoidable crisis and put an end to the terrible uncertainty that overwhelmed the human race.[19]

During such a celebration, statues of gods were removed from their places in temples, mounted on wagons or boats, and paraded through the city.

Moreover, Sumerians became more thoughtful about broad and philosophical questions: How did the universe begin? What is the greatest power? What is good, and what is evil? Their stories and their views of the gods reveal how they thought. Formerly known as the "heaven god," An became the symbol of greatest power; he ruled the gods and settled disputes. Enlil, the air god, came to be worshiped as the creator of the world and master of humanity, the god who chose the rulers. Enki, the water god, became the god of intelligence and wisdom, the "broad-eared" one who knew the name of everything, the one who protected the arts, science, literature, and magicians. He became the ear and mind of the whole land. The sun god, Utu, took on powers to reward human goodness and wickedness; it was he who punished wicked humans by sending the Flood.

The Universe and Its Creation

Scholars have analyzed Sumerian myths and stories to determine the people's vision of the universe and how it was created. Sumerians saw the earth as a flat disk surrounded by mountains. In the center of the flat disk, or Mesopotamia, was the city of Nippur. Resting on outlying mountains was the dome of the sky. A substance called *lil*, a word that means "wind," perhaps suggesting air or breath or spirit, filled the space between the earth and sky. Beneath the earth lay the netherworld, the place inhabited by the dead. During the day, the sun traced an arc across the sky dome; at night it lit the underworld on its way to the starting place to begin another day. Around all—from the top of the sky dome to the bottom of the netherworld and on all sides—was a boundless sea, which kept the universe in place.

In the beginning, they believed, there was only a sea. Out of this primeval sea came the heaven, which covered the flat earth like a rounded lid, and the atmosphere in between earth and sky. Out of this atmosphere, the *lil*, came sun, moon, planets, and stars. After the creation of those bodies, plants, animals, and humans appeared on the earth. The gods did the creating. A tablet listing Sumerian gods shows the goddess Nammu, who is symbolized by the pictograph used for the primeval sea; it also describes her as the mother, the one who gave birth to heaven and earth. Out of the union of heaven, An, and earth, Ki, was born Enlil, the air god. The union between Enlil and Ki made possible the design and creation of the rest of the universe. Creation was a three-part process: making a plan, giving the word to create, and naming the thing created. This three-part model for creation became the doctrine throughout the Ancient Near East; the same sequence is described in the creation story later told in Genesis in the Hebrew Bible.

From very early times the people believed in an afterlife, as suggested by the

A detail from a cylinder-seal shows a man facing Nergal, god of pestilence and death. The Sumerians believed that many gods ruled all aspects of earthly activity.

practice of leaving food vessels and objects with the dead. Stories written in the age of dynasties expand on the initial idea. Ruled over by Ereshkigal and Nergal, her husband, the place of afterlife was a land of no return, under the ground. To get there, the dead took off their clothes and crossed a river. Lines from the poem *The Epic of Gilgamesh* describe the place called the House of Darkness as seen in a dream:

> To the house which none leave who have entered it,
> On the road from which there is no way back,
> To the house wherein the dwellers are bereft of light,
> Where dust is their fare and clay their food.
> They are clothed like birds, with wings for garments,
> And see no light, residing in darkness.
> In the House of Dust, which I entered,

I looked at [rulers], their crowns put away;
I [saw princes], those (born to) the crown,
Who had ruled the land from the days of yore.[20]

This place was the afterlife for all people; the Sumerians did not envision a perfect place for some and a horrible place for others.

Though the people had long believed that the gods had created humans as earthly servants for divine beings, beliefs about the relationship between humans and gods became more complex during the period of the dynasties. First, the priests took on a new role. Besides having charge of festivals and rituals, they interceded between individuals and the gods. A person could also ask for help from his or her tutelary god, who stood nearby like a guardian angel. Second, the Sumerians thought the gods had come up with additional duties for their worshipers: People still had to send offerings to the temples and attend religious ceremonies, but they also were required to live by the gods' rules of ethics and avoid the gods' taboos (prohibited behaviors). The precepts, or rules, for a good life required them to be good parents, sons, and neighbors and to practice kindness, compassion, righteousness, and sincerity. Third, Sumerians no longer believed that good crops were the only reward for good behavior. They also came to expect comfort in distress, honorable social position, numerous children, and great wealth. On the other hand, Sumerians believed that violators of the rules might be punished by the gods. In these ways, religion was more complex than it had been in the days before the dynasties.

Sumerian Art

Like religion, art advanced during the age of expansion, as revealed by the many art objects of high quality found in the excavations. Tablets tell of singers in temples, music lessons in schools, and songs and dances performed to entertain people in the marketplace and in homes. Musical instruments found in the Ur tombs suggest that music was part of the burial ceremony. Lyres, harps, tambourines, and metal and reed pipes (wind instruments like recorders or flutes) lay buried in the rubble of palaces and temples. Beautifully designed cylinder-seals, the Mesopotamian trademark, depict worshipers and gods, as well as kings on battlefields and shepherds defending cattle. Though Sumer had no mines, Sumerian metalworkers became

Artists thrived during Mesopotamia's expansion period. (Left) This tablet from 3000 B.C. features musicians playing various instruments. (Right) A beautiful sculpture dating from 3000 B.C. depicts a goat inlaid with gold and lapis lazuli.

highly skilled in the crafting of imported materials. A copper chariot pulled by four onagers (wild asses) shows that artisans had learned to cast metal. A he-goat statue, mounted on a wooden frame and symbolizing plant and animal fertility, shows how artisans combined gold, silver, and lapis lazuli (a semiprecious stone in shades of blue). The artist who created the hammered gold helmet found in the Ur tomb made fine lines in the gold to represent individual hairs. Cast in bronze, a life-size head of a king has a realistic face and a detailed beard. Hundreds of art objects indicate that Sumerians appreciated beauty and recognized that the expression of the human spirit was important.

Sumerian artists were at their best with sculpture, which conveyed emotion and spirit. In temples throughout Mesopotamia, Sumerians left hundreds of votive statues (figurines symbolizing a wish or prayer) in hopes that the statues would intercede for them with the gods. Some of these works are incompletely carved in stone. One shows a seated couple holding hands. A group of statues from the latter part of the Early Dynastic period shows a characteristic male, with long hair parted in the middle, a squared beard, and a fringed wool skirt held up by a girdle, or belt. The eyes in these statues are inlays of shell or lapis lazuli. A later statue shows Ebih-il, an official from the city of Mari, seated with hands folded in prayer. He wears a *kaunakes*, a Sumerian garment made of overlapping wool tufts. Another statue shows a woman whose dress is a

Sumerians were especially adept at sculpture. At right is a votive statue, symbolizing a wish or a prayer. Such a statue would be left at a temple in the hope that the statue would intercede with the gods on behalf of its owner. At left is a sculpture of Ebih-il, an official from the city of Mari, hands folded in prayer.

A piece of the Stele of the Vultures (top left) shows soldiers marching in phalanx. Scenes from the royal standard of Ur portray war (bottom) and peace (top right).

long piece of fabric wrapped around her, leaving one shoulder bare.

Sumerian artists also made many fine steles. A stele is a stone or a slab that stands upright; its surface bears words or a sculpted design carved in relief, usually commemorating an important event. The earlier steles had more than one register, or line of drawings. On one, Ur-Nanshe, king of Lagash, commemorates temple building; the top register shows him and his children building, and on the lower register they are seen celebrating the completion of their work. The Stele of the Vultures commemorates the victory of a battle. On the top register, soldiers march in phalanx; on the lower register, the leader drives a chariot. In the royal tomb at Ur, excavators found the "royal standard," which is like a stele but made with inlay rather than sculpture. One side shows many figures and scenes of battle; the other side, depicting peace, shows scenes from banquets and agricultural activities. A later stele shows a victory celebrated on a mountain with the leader protected by symbols of gods. Some steles have holes in them, indicating that they had been hung on walls for decoration. All these steles show the fine artistic skills achieved by Sumerian sculptors.

Sumerian Literature

Of all the arts, literature is perhaps the Sumerians' finest achievement. Scholars have classified Sumerian literature into eight categories: myths, epic tales, hymns, lamentations, historiographic documents, essays, precepts (rules of conduct), and proverbs. Sumerian literature was translated and copied throughout the Ancient Near East, and it influenced both Hebrew and Greek writers.

Among the many myths, three are similar to stories later told in the Old Testament. As entertainers in royal palaces, minstrels created and sang secular (nonreligious) myths. Only later did scribes record them. One myth tells a story about humans, who had been created from clay and lived in a pure land called Dilmun, where there was no sickness or death, but also no fresh water. Enki orders fresh water brought up from the earth, like the stream that came up in the Garden of Eden, and Dilmun turns into a divine garden. The myth tells of a female offering Enki plants that bring a curse and cause

sickness to his rib. Then a "Lady of the Rib" is created to heal it. Another myth, similar to the biblical story of Noah, tells about Ziusudra, a good man who listens at a wall and overhears that Enki has decided to send a flood. Like Noah, he builds a boat and survives the flood, and when the waters have receded, he praises Utu, the sun god, for coming back, to light and warm the earth.

In a poem essay, a Sumerian writer addresses the same dilemma of human suffering faced by Job in the biblical story written many years later. The older essay tells of a good and god-fearing man who, like Job in the more familiar story, also loses his possessions and suffers greatly. In the end, both men are returned to health and have their possessions restored. Like Job, the man in the essay cries out to his god during his suffering:

> My god, (I would stand) before you,
> Would speak to you, . . . , my word is a groan,
> I would tell you about it, would bemoan the bitterness of my path,
> (Would bewail) the confusion of. . . .
> Lo, let not my mother who bore me cease my lament before you.
> Let not my sister utter the happy song and chant.
> Let her utter tearfully my misfortunes before you,
> Let my wife voice mournfully my suffering,
> Let the expert singer bemoan my bitter fate.
> My god, the day shines bright over the land, for me the day is black.[21]

The epic poem is the greatest Sumerian literary invention. So far nine have been found, but one stands out as the best. Put together from separate hero stories about the most famous king of Erech, *The Epic of Gilgamesh* is a single poem of eleven tablets or parts. Unlike a conventional novel, this work of literature places several tales together, unified by the character of Gilgamesh. Though gods have roles in the story, Gilgamesh holds the spotlight in the series of episodes. Translator E. A. Speiser says of the poem: "For the first time in the history of the world a profound experience on such a heroic scale has found expression in a noble style. The scope and sweep of the epic, and its sheer poetic power, give it a timeless appeal."[22] The poem is timeless because it involves the hero in problems common to all humans—friendship, loyalty, the urge to be famous, love of adventure, fear of death, and the longing to be immortal.

In the story a brave and proud Gilgamesh meets a peasant named Enkidu; the two become friends and go on adventures. They slay a monster in the cedar forest and kill a bull sent by a god. For his part in slaying the monster and the bull, Enkidu must die. For twelve days the condemned man is sick, and Gilgamesh, unable to help, suffers because of the illness and death of his friend. Sad and alone, Gilgamesh sets out to find the secret to eternal life. He seeks out Utanapishtim, the wise king who survived the Flood, but the wise king has few encouraging words. Urged by his wife, Utanapishtim tells Gilgamesh where to find the plant of eternal youth at the bottom of the sea. Gilgamesh goes diving, finds the plant, and happily looks forward to his return to Erech. But the gods have other plans. When Gilgamesh goes bathing, a snake takes the plant away, and Gilgamesh goes back to Erech, tired and disappointed.

Hundreds of other tablets record the other kinds of literature. There are temple

An impression made by a cylinder-seal shows Gilgamesh fighting two lions. The Epic of Gilgamesh *is a wonderful example of one of early Sumer's greatest literary contributions, the epic poem.*

Gilgamesh Mourns

The greatness of The Epic of Gilgamesh *lies in its portrayal of feelings common to all readers. When his friend Enkidu dies, Gilgamesh grieves. This following excerpt from the poem comes from a translation in Volume 1 of James B. Pritchard's anthology* The Ancient Near East.

"Hear me, O elders [and give ear] unto me!
It is for Enkidu, my [friend], that I weep,
Moaning bitterly like a wailing woman.
The axe at my side, my hand's trust,
The dirk in my belt, [the shield] in front of me,
My festal robe, my richest trimming—
an evil [demon] rose up and robbed me,
[O my younger friend], thou chasedst
The wild ass of the hills, the panther of the steppe!
Enkidu, my younger friend, thou who chasedst
The wild ass of the hills, the panther of the steppe!
We who [have conquered] all things, scaled [the mountains],
Who seized the Bull [and slew him],
Brought affliction on [the monster] Hubaba, who [dwelled in the Cedar Forest]!
What, now, is this sleep that has laid hold [on thee]?
Thou art benighted [in the dark] and canst not hear [me]!"
But he lifts not up [his eyes];
He touched his heart, but it does not beat.
Then he veiled (his) friend like a bride[. . .],
Storming over him like a lion,
Like a lioness deprived of [her] whelps.
He paces back and forth before [*the couch*],

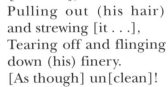

Pulling out (his hair) and strewing [it . . .],
Tearing off and flinging down (his) finery.
[As though] un[clean]!

A Babylonian sculpture depicts a scene from the life of Gilgamesh.

hymns praising the gods and glorifying the temples. There are lamentations (sad songs) mourning the destruction of cities, the loss of wealth, and the death of loved ones. Other literature gives rules for living and working, like the "farmer's almanac." Hundreds of tablets record proverbs, which students copied over and over in school to learn cuneiform. Examples include "Marry a wife according to your choice; have a child as your heart desires," and "Friendship lasts a day; kinship endures forever."[23] Sumerians loved debate and recorded arguments between two opposing sides, usually personified as animals, plants, seasons, or tools. And, finally, historiography tells stories of battles, their victories and defeats. All the forms of Sumerian literature have been found in other parts of the Ancient Near East; other cultures sometimes copied the works exactly and sometimes revised them to fit their own peoples.

Invasion by Sargon

Conflicts had occurred among the city-states in Sumer since the first king of Kish had come to dominate the region, but the kings had been more interested in advancing the civilization than in entering conflicts to expand the territory. Thus far, kings had always been Sumerian kings. Eventually, an outsider, a Semite, became the king of Kish. The word *Semite* comes from Sem, or Shem, one of the sons of Noah, who supposedly was the ancestor of Assyrian, Aramaean, and Hebrew people. Semitic people had lived in Sumerian cities from the beginning, but they were the minority. In 2370 B.C., after twenty-five

Sargon of Akkad took control of Mesopotamia in 2370 B.C., ending the Early Dynastic period.

hundred years of Sumerian rule in southern Mesopotamia, Sargon of Akkad took control. Akkad was the home of a group of Semitic people who lived in the central part of Mesopotamia, from the Nippur region north. They had an agricultural way of life almost identical to that in Sumer, except that their language was different. The name "Akkadian" came to stand for all the non-Sumerian people of Mesopotamia.

When Sargon of Akkad came to power, the Early Dynastic period ended. Sargon,

Sumerian Proverbs

We are doomed to die, let us spend;

We will live long, let us save.

The poor man is better dead than alive;
If he has bread, he has no salt,
If he has salt, he has no bread,
If he has meat, he has no lamb
If he has a lamb, he has no meat.

Who possesses much silver may be happy,
who possesses much barley may be happy,
But who has nothing at all can sleep.
I am a thoroughbred steed,
But I am hitched to a mule
And must draw a cart,
And carry reeds and stubble.

Who has not supported a wife or child
His nose has not borne a leash.

The ox plows,
The dog spoils the deep furrows.

The smith's dog could not overturn the anvil;
He (therefore) overturned the waterpot instead.

He did not yet catch the fox,
Yet he is making a neck-stock [stiff collar] for it.

Upon my escaping from the wild ox,
The wild cow confronted me.

Hand and hand, a man's house is built;
Stomach and stomach, a man's house is destroyed.

Who builds like a lord, lives like a slave;
Who builds like a slave, lives like a lord.

You go and carry off the enemy's land;
The enemy comes and carries off your land.

You can have a lord, you can have a king,
But the man to fear is the "governor."

whose reign lasted for fifty-five years, came from humble beginnings. According to legend, kind peasants brought him up because he was an orphan. He became the cupbearer for Ur-Zababa, king of Kish, but he overthrew his master and became king. Sargon marched his army against Uruk (Erech) and then Ur, Lagash, and Umma until he had taken all the city-states to the southern border and had "washed his weapons in the Lower Sea."[24] He founded a new capital in Agade, installed Akkadian governors in the Sumerian cities, and made the Akkadian language official for all administration.

When Sargon had established political and moral authority over Sumer, he launched military campaigns east to Susa, the capital of Elam, and north toward Syria, Nineveh, and Anatolia, far enough to gain access to the cedar forest in Lebanon and precious metals in the mountains. His successful campaigns created for the first time a Mesopotamian empire, which reached the limits of the known world. Sargon's realm was also called the Akkadian Empire. For the first time, a king ruling Sumer had cared less about Sumerian traditions and more about gaining territory. Nonetheless, the same religion, art, and customs continued. Sargon's sons and grandson succeeded him and ruled the empire for another sixty-one years, but it collapsed after the grandson's death.

The Third Dynasty of Ur

Conflict had begun slowly in Sumer as city-states fought for supremacy, and conflict continued as Sargon took over one city-state after another. According to Quigley's seven-stage model, a civilization that involves itself in conflict and war will continue to decline and will begin to decay unless it returns to the third stage, expansion, and invests again in inventions. Sumer returned to the stage of expansion, at least briefly, after the collapse of the Akkadian Empire. At this time the king of Uruk, supported by other Sumerian kings, launched a rebellion against the would-be successors of Sargon's grandson. During the revolt, Ur-Nammu replaced the king of Uruk, and completed the liberation. It was Ur-Nammu who founded the great Third Dynasty of Ur, which lasted more than a hundred years under five kings. As king of Ur, and of Sumer and Akkad as well, Ur-Nammu began a period of peace and prosperity and a rebirth of art and literature.

Ur became the capital of a great empire, a city, as archaeologist Leonard Woolley states, "worthy of its political preeminence, . . . crowded with magnificent monuments testifying to the wealth and piety of its kings."[25] Ur-Nammu embarked on a building program that his son finished. First, he surrounded the city with a wall and a moat on three sides, leaving only one dry-land approach. Then he built or rebuilt a complex of buildings around the ziggurat, which now featured hanging gardens with a drainage system of "weeper-holes" to keep the interior dry. At the gateway leading to the terrace of the ziggurat, Ur-Nammu built the House of Tablets, which served as a law court and the center of the temple's business. He built storerooms and a temple. He built the royal palace and the royal mausoleum, the tombs Woolley excavated. He had steles made; the best was the one of war

A relief shows Ur-Nammu offering a sacrifice to the god Sin. Ur-Nammu founded the great Third Dynasty of Ur, which lasted more than a hundred years.

and peace found in the tomb. Woolley sums up the grandeur of Ur this way:

> Ur as the capital of the empire could command the best, and we may well imagine that no former age in Sumer had produced buildings so vast, combining such solid strength with an architectural *finesse* unequaled un-til the Greek period and, probably, with a wealth of ornament that no previous Sumerian ruler could have afforded.[26]

The Third Dynasty of Ur ended when the Elamites invaded the city from the east (modern Iran), sacked it, and burned it down.

5 Conflict: Imperial Wars, 2500–800 B.C.

A civilization that spends its wealth on luxury and war and neglects its economic growth and its people gradually declines, although strong and concerned rulers may bring about brief upswings. The peace and prosperity experienced in Sumer with the return to stage three expansion lasted but a short time. Conflict began again, setting off a period of imperial wars that lasted nearly two thousand years.

The grandeur of the Third Dynasty of Ur was maintained through the first half of the reign of Ur-Nammu's son Shulgi,

Mesopotamian warriors square off in a relief from 3000 B.C. War and excessive luxury eventually depleted the treasuries of Sumerian civilization and led to a period of decline.

the second of five kings in this dynasty. During the first half of his forty-seven-year reign, Shulgi completed the buildings his father had started and built new ones. He reinstated gods in their shrines and reformed the calendar. During the second half, however, he undertook military campaigns against small towns to the north and east of Ur. Since these places posed little threat, there seemed to be no need for numerous campaigns, but the historical records offer no explanation.

Shulgi called himself the King of the Four Quarters (of the World) and had himself worshiped as a god. His son Amar-Sin was even more arrogant. Though he built temples and fought battles, he called himself "the god who gives life to the country" or "the god sun of the Land." Amar-Sin's reign ended abruptly when, according to an omen-text (the record of a person especially skilled at interpreting signs or omens) he died of an infection caused by a "shoe-bite," probably an infected blister from a shoe. Shulgi and his son ruled over an empire as large as the Akkadian Empire of Sargon but better managed because these kings built roads and safe stopping places for administrators traveling to the outlying cities.

The last two kings in the dynasty continued to involve themselves in war. Shu-Sin, Amar-Sin's brother, restored temples, but he also continued military efforts. Shu-Sin particularly hated the Semite, or Syrian, tribes called the Amorites or MAR.TU, nomads who invaded the king's territory to graze their herds. Archaeologist Georges Roux quotes an old Sumerian text, which describes them with contempt:

The MAR.TU who know no grain. . . .
The MAR.TU who know no house nor town, the boors [slobs] of the mountains. . . . The MAR.TU who digs up truffles [an edible tuberous plant] . . . who does not bend his knees (to cultivate land), who eats raw meat, who has no house during his lifetime, who is not buried after his death.[27]

Because the nomads raided towns and attacked caravans on the roads, Shu-Sin ordered police actions against them and occasionally launched military raids and took the Amorites as prisoners of war. As a defense, Shu-Sin built a fortress to the north, between Ur and Mari.

The Fall of Ur

After Shu-Sin died and his son Ibbi-Sin became king, the state of the dynasty deteriorated. After years of spending large amounts of money on war, the kings had left the people poor and starving, and one by one cities began to revolt against the central government in Ur. In addition, the MAR.TU increased pressure on towns and on the borders; they cut off roads leading to Ur, and an Amorite became king at Larsa, only twenty-five miles from Ur. Then the Elamites from the east invaded Sumer. To save his kingdom, Ibbi-Sin tried to make an alliance with the Amorites against the Elamites, but it was too late. The Elamites had reached the walls of Ur. They invaded the city, stole everything valuable, burned down the buildings, and took Ibbi-Sin prisoner. Ur had fallen.

The fall of Ur, in 2006 B.C., was significant. Historically, it marked a major turning point: the end of a dynasty, the end of an empire, and the end of Sumer as a rul-

The Destruction of Ur

When the Elamites destroyed Ur, the Sumerians felt the loss as a national catastrophe and recorded their sadness in a lamentation. In Ancient Iraq, *archaeologist Georges Roux quotes historian Samuel Noah Kramer's translation of the poem.*

O Father Nanna, that city into ruins was made . . .
Its people, not potsherds [broken pieces of pottery], filled its sides;
Its walls were breached; the people groan.
In its lofty gates, where they were wont [accustomed] to promenade, dead bodies were lying about;
In its boulevards, where the feasts were celebrated, scattered they lay.
In all its streets, where they were wont to promenade, dead bodies were lying about;
In its places, where the festivities of the land took place, the people lay in heaps . . .
Ur—its weak and its strong perished through hunger;
Mothers and fathers who did not leave their houses were overcome by fire;
The young lying on their mothers' laps, like fish were carried off by the waters;
In the city, the wife was abandoned, the son was abandoned, the possessions were scattered about.
O Nanna, Ur has been destroyed, its people have been dispersed!

ing nation. In the evolution of civilizations, the events in Ur mark a shift from expansion to conflict and early decay. When leaders stop investing surplus wealth in the society and spend it on war and luxury instead, they lose the people's loyalty. The Third Dynasty of Ur failed finally for several reasons. First, Ibbi-Sin's officials revolted and the city-states seceded, making administration difficult, if not impossible. Second, the king's forces were spread too thin as he tried to defend his towns and roads against widespread Amorite attacks. And, third, the Elamites took the capital city. In time the Elamites were expelled, but the Semites stayed and ruled for many centuries.

During the next two centuries in Mesopotamia, small and large kingdoms fought for control, but none emerged as ruler of the entire area. In the south, the kingdoms of Isin and Larsa fought for control of Sumer and Akkad; in the north Mari and Assur fought to control the trade routes. In the meantime Semitic tribes of nomads moved in and started their own little kingdoms around towns. Gone were the city-states ruled by Enlil's chosen kings; in their places were kings who had acquired power by conquest and military victory.

The Isin-Larsa Period

During the first part of the Isin-Larsa period, Isin overshadowed Larsa. King Ishbi-Irra of Isin brought Nippur, Uruk, and Eridu under his control and captured Ur from the Elamites; later, his grandson added Sippar. Then the king of Larsa attacked Isin and occupied Ur; when he also took Lagash, Susa, and Uruk, he proclaimed himself ruler of Sumer and Akkad. Every time Ur was attacked and destroyed, victors or other rulers restored the important city—rebuilt the wall, the temples, the palaces, and other buildings. Woolley's excavations from the Isin-Larsa and other periods of rebuilding in Ur provide information about technology, about common people's housing and way of life, and about changes in burial customs.

Woolley's excavations uncovered parts of the city wall and a temple kitchen, both showing advances in technology. One part of the wall, the rampart, had been built so strongly that neither the Elamites nor time had destroyed it. Woolley discovered that it had been built wide enough to contain houses and temples. The ground floor had no openings toward the outside, but the levels above had windows on both sides. Parts of the wall were wide enough for a chariot. In the debris, Woolley also found a sizable kitchen, which would have been needed to feed the large temple staff. The kitchen had a well and a waterproof tank and, against one wall, two fireplaces for boiling water. Against another wall stood a cutting table made of brick, the marks of the butcher's knife still visible. Woolley goes on to explain:

> In a side-room was the beehive-shaped oven for baking bread, and in another room the cooking-range with two furnaces and circular flues, and in the flat top of it rings of small holes where the cauldrons were to be set; after thirty-eight centuries one could yet light the fires and reconstruct with all its activities the temple kitchen of the seventeenth century before Christ.[28]

Homes of middle-class people stood along narrow, winding streets. At every corner, the builders had rounded the bricks so that people would not catch their clothes or scrape their arms on sharp edges. Each house had a door that opened in, but there were no windows on the ground floor. Residents of these houses dumped all their trash onto the street, and the narrow lanes rose higher and higher. When the street was higher than a family's doorstep, the family moved the doorsill up. When the trash was so high that the door was useless, they tore down the house and built a new one with a proper door. The streets had drains for water, but apparently the idea of garbage removal never occurred to anyone.

Inside the door of a middle-class home, steps led down to a small room equipped with a drain and a jug of water for washing feet. A second door led into the house; against the doorjamb hung a mask of the god Puzuzu, a charm to protect the family from the southwest wind, which, Sumerians thought, brought fever. The house was built around a courtyard with doors leading to rooms on both the ground floor and the floor above. The kitchen, store-

Excavations from Ur have shown that during the period of about 2000 B.C., people lived in comfortable homes with furniture such as this bed and chair.

rooms, and slave quarters were on the ground floor, and the family living quarters were upstairs. Excavations show that these homes also had indoor rooms with toilets. Little was left of furnishings, but cylinder-seals suggest that Sumerians used folding chairs and tables, wood and wicker storage chests, and many-colored rugs.

Each house had its own shrine and its own burial place, middle-class versions of the chapels and tombs in royal palaces. In a tomb vault located behind the guest rooms at the back of the house, each family buried its dead. By keeping the remains in the house, the people ensured that deceased family members were not forgotten and cut off from their descendants. The family shrine had an altar and an incense hearth for worship of the family's tutelary god, whose name was the same as the family name. Both the shrine and the burial place signify a change in customs. In earlier times, the temple had been the center of public ceremony and ritual. When

monarchy (the system of kingship) had become more important than the priesthood, religion and ritual became more personal and private.

Power Struggles in the North

In the north, the kingdoms of Assur and Mari had the most power, but neither city could make a nation of the northern cities or an empire of the whole region. The two cities were similar in many ways. Both were old, already established by the Early Dynastic period, around 2625 B.C., and both had been under the cultural influence of Sumer. Since both developed the same religion and temple system as the cities in Sumer, each had its own temple dedicated to Ishtar, the fertility goddess, who corresponded to Inanna, the goddess of love of the Early Dynastic period of Ur. Both cities lay on trade routes: Assur was located on the Tigris and Mari on the Euphrates. During the Isin-Larsa period, both extended their kingdoms, Assur north to Nineveh and Mari west to the Mediterranean, and both cities had as much trouble with invading Semitic tribes as did the cities in the south. Yet, each city had important features of its own. Assur had natural barriers on three sides of the city; a bend in the river bounded two sides and a mountain the third, giving Assur protection from invaders. Mari, a city that had already produced many fine pieces of art, had a beautiful royal palace; in its rooms were found tablets recording the varied activities of kings.

The balance of power remained about the same until the arrival of the Amorites, who came from Syria and the western desert. Historian Joan Oates describes their beginning:

> In 1894 BC an Amorite dynasty was founded at Babylon which was to bring that city to a pre-eminence it maintained, psychologically if not politically, for nearly 2000 years. Up to this time, . . . Babylon had made no mark on its country's history. Yet little over 100 years later this city ruled all Mesopotamia, albeit briefly.[29]

Hammurabi

A king named Hammurabi, the sixth of eleven kings in the dynasty, eliminated all rival kings whose kingdoms had been vying for control of the region for more than two centuries. When he had unified Sumer and Akkad and had extended his rule to Assyria in the northwest corner, he made Babylon the capital and Babylonia

Hammurabi's takeover of Sumer and Akkad led to the rise of the Babylonians and the end of Sumerian rule.

the new name for the unified region. The rise of the Babylonians marked the end of the Sumerians as a political, ethnic, and linguistic entity.

Hammurabi was a great Mesopotamian monarch who achieved his goal with a special strategy and hard work. Thirty to forty thousand tablets found in Mari and in southern cities and fifty-five of Hammurabi's letters tell about his activities and the changes that took place during his reign. As a descendant of an Amorite sheik (leader of a village), Hammurabi inherited a small kingdom eighty miles long and twenty miles wide, surrounded by larger kingdoms. He developed this small kingdom of Babylon into an empire by using patience and consideration. When he came to power in 1792 B.C., he waited five years before taking any action to expand. Then he spent twenty years remodeling temples and fortifying

A trial takes place before Hammurabi. Hammurabi established consistent punishments for wrongdoing in a series of 282 laws called the Code of Hammurabi.

towns to gain the trust of the people. During these years, Mari joined with Babylon. Hammurabi was a skillful diplomat who conveyed a genuine concern for his subjects' welfare. He respected the people's gods and their traditions and made no effort to enforce the worship of new gods or the use of unfamiliar practices. In the twenty-ninth year of his reign, he started attacking. A skilled military leader, he conquered four out of five kingdoms in ten years and formed them under one Babylonian rule. He attacked Mari, the city that joined with Babylon, but he did not conquer Elam, which had been rebuilt. By waiting and building, he had prepared his way for success.

Hammurabi had a clear idea of the responsibilities of a ruler; he tended to administrative, diplomatic, legal, and military matters as well as to trivial concerns. He gave clear orders, listened to and encouraged those who worked for him, and punished those who did wrong. He appointed capable officials and involved himself in clearing and digging canals and other public works. As a diplomat he exchanged presents with other royal men and lis-

tened to them. He mobilized troops. Yet, his law code reveals that he attended to small matters, too.

Life During Hammurabi's Rule

By the time Hammurabi ruled, the temples and gods were important only in the religious and social life of the city people; the royal palace managed the Babylonian economy. Temples were complexes of many buildings, usually with a courtyard where statues were set up for feast days. Around the courtyard were living quarters, libraries, schools for priests, workshops, and storerooms. Another courtyard had an altar. A three-room temple, which only priests could enter, had an inner room, the holy of holies, where a statue of the temple's god stood. Every day there was a temple ceremony—music, hymns, or prayers. Every day people brought food to the god's table, such as bread, cakes, honey, and fruit, and libations, such as water, wine, or beer. The flesh of animals

Letters from Mari

In Letters from Mesopotamia, *historian A. Leo Oppenheim has translated official and private correspondence found in the palace in Mari. Two from the collection illustrate the tone and concerns of Babylonians of nearly four thousand years ago.*

"Tell my lord: Your servant Yarim-Addu sends the following message:

Two officials of King Ḫammurapi, Tāb-eli-mātim and Sin-bēl-aplim, who for a long time were staying in the city Maškanšabra, have arrived here in Babylon; four men from Larsa, riding on donkeys, are escorting them. I obtained intelligence [information] of the message they are carrying (from the king of Larsa); they are supposed to tell (Ḫammurapi) the following: 'As to the soldiers for whom you keep writing me, the reason why I did not send them to you is that I have heard that the enemy's intentions are directed against another country. But I am still holding the soldiers in readiness; should the enemy turn against you, my soldiers will come to your aid. On the other hand should the enemy turn against me, your soldiers should come to my aid.' This is the message which King Rim-Sin (of Larsa) sent to Ḫammurapi (of Babylon)."

"Tell my lord: Your servant Yakim-Addu sends the following message:

A short time ago I wrote to my lord as follows: 'A lion was caught in the loft of a house in Akkaka. My lord should write me whether this lion should remain in that same loft until the arrival of my lord, or whether I should have it brought to my lord.' But letters from my lord were slow in coming and the lion has been in the loft for five days. Although they threw him a dog and a pig, he refused to eat them. I was worrying: 'Heaven forbid that this lion pine away.' I became scared, but eventually I got the lion into a wooden cage and loaded it on a boat to have it brought to my lord."

burned on the altar, and smoke from cedar and cypress wood filled the air. People came seeking help for their troubles, or they asked priests to read omens and tell their future. The temples in the various cities served people in many social ways as well as being the official homes of the city gods.

The royal palace excavated at Mari perhaps best illustrates the grand living kings had set up for themselves. In the early days in Sumerian city-states, leaders dwelt in modest buildings. The royal palace in Mari, however, was like a city within a city, with apartments, reception rooms, a throne room, offices, workshops, stores, and courtyards surrounded by thick walls. The palace covered seven acres. It was well constructed of fine materials and was decorated beautifully with white plaster floors, statues of princes, and wall paintings of figures from Sumerian mythology. Upon excavation, two terracotta bathrooms were still in place. The king and queen had their own private chapels. The servants' quarters and the maintenance system took three hundred rooms. The palace grounds had a drainage system built with brick gutters and bitumen-lined clay pipes installed thirty feet underground. During excavation, there was a drenching rainstorm, and the system, still working after forty centuries of disuse, drained the site in a few hours.

In contrast, ordinary citizens lived in crowded communities where streets wound around without plan. Little shops and bazaars mixed with houses. From open-air stalls, peddlers sold food, clothes, rugs, pots, spices, and perfumes. Stands selling bowls of prepared onions and cucumbers, fried fish, or grilled meat stood next to the blacksmith shop. There was little traffic, since the streets were too narrow for carts or even a donkey carrying a wide load. On a regular day, servants shopped and carried water, a storyteller recited "Gilgamesh" at the crossroads, and children ran to and from school two or three times a day.

Besides uniting the kingdoms into one, Hammurabi kept most of the old traditions. By the time of his rule, much temple land had already been transferred into private hands, and city governors and assemblies managed petty affairs and collected taxes. Hammurabi did, however, make one major religious change. He made Marduk the head of the gods, replacing Enlil, and gave Marduk the qualities of the other gods. He rewrote the creation epic and named Marduk the creator. And Hammurabi contributed the extensive code of laws that bears his name.

The Code of Hammurabi was not the first written system of laws, however. Archaeologists found a tablet from the beginning of the Third Dynasty of Ur, recording laws of Ur-Nammu. Ur-Nammu had tried to make the punishment fit the crime by imposing fines for lesser offenses, rather than death or physical injury. According to archaeologist Georges Roux, this practice "is the sign of a society far more polished and civilized than is usually imagined."[30]

Hammurabi's Laws

Toward the end of his reign, Hammurabi recorded his laws on steles of basalt (a hard, dark rock), to be placed in temples. One shows Hammurabi praying before a seated god—Marduk, or Shamash, the sun god, also the god of justice—carved in relief on the top. One eight-foot stele, now in the Louvre, France's national art museum in Paris, has the laws carved in forty-nine cuneiform columns. In the prologue to the laws, Hammurabi said he wanted "justice to prevail in the country/To de-

Hammurabi's Laws

Hammurabi wrote his 282 laws by describing various conditions and then telling what should follow. Anthologist James B. Pritchard includes Theophile Meek's translation of the entire code. A few examples serve to illustrate the range of topics and the severity of punishments.

"6: If a seignior [any free man of standing] stole the property of church or state, that seignior shall be put to death; also the one who received the stolen goods from his hand shall be put to death. . . .

59: If a seignior cut down a tree in a(nother) seignior's orchard without the consent of the owner of the orchard, he shall pay one-half mina of silver. . . .

127: If a seignior pointed the finger at a nun or the wife of a(nother) seignior, but has proved nothing, they shall drag that seignior into the presence of the judges and also cut off half his (hair).

128: If a seignior acquired a wife, but did not draw up contracts for her, that woman is no wife. . . .

153: If a seignior's wife has brought about the death of her husband because of another man, they shall impale that woman on stakes. . . .

205: If a seignior's slave has struck the cheek of a member of the aristocracy, they shall cut off his ear. . . .

218: If a physician performed a major operation on a seignior with a bronze lancet and has caused the seignior's death, or he opened up the eye-socket of a seignior and has destroyed the seignior's eye, they shall cut off his hand. . . .

248: If a seignior hired an ox and has broken its horn, cut off its tail, or injured the flesh of its back, he shall give one-quarter its value in silver. . . .

282: If a male slave has said to his master, 'You are not my master,' his master shall prove him to be his slave and cut off his ear."

stroy the wicked and the evil,/That the strong may not oppress the weak." [31] Two hundred eighty-two laws give rules and the punishments for their violations. The criminal code is based on the concept of "an eye for an eye." Other laws cover the sale of goods and slaves, stealing, the behavior of soldiers, owners and tenants, savings and borrowing, marriages and divorces, inheritance, doctors and veterinarians, and the hire of boats, animals, and people. In the epilogue to the laws,

(Left) Hammurabi's eight-foot stele that contains the text of his laws. At right is a close-up of the top of the stele that depicts Hammurabi receiving his laws from the god of justice.

Hammurabi wrote that he had indeed fulfilled his goal.

The so-called Old Babylonian Empire ended shortly after Hammurabi's death in 1750 B.C. Though Babylonian rule had spelled the end of Sumer as a political entity, indirectly Hammurabi had extended Sumerian influence because the Babylonians had adopted Sumerian culture and spread it farther. The well-developed business and legal systems remained in place after Hammurabi's death, but the arts declined. Nearly a half-century of a centralized rule by force had weakened and demoralized the provinces, and the people there revolted, leaving the kingdom disintegrated and Babylon a minor capital city. In the absence of leadership, Mesopotamia was in disarray, and other tribes soon took advantage of this condition.

6 Influence and Conflict: Mesopotamia and Its Neighbors, 1750–800 B.C.

While the major early civilizations developed in Egypt and Sumeria, a menagerie of tribes and nations occupied the northern part of the Fertile Crescent south to the border of Egypt. At various times tribes conflicted with the major civilizations, but the influence of these early superpowers was always present. Although Sumerian culture primarily defined the customs and values of the lesser tribes, they had characteristics of their own, and several made important contributions.

The Hittites

The Hittites, from Asia Minor, or Anatolia, were a non-Semitic people whose language had combined with that of invaders from southern Europe who spoke an Indo-European tongue. They developed an empire between 2000 and 1500 B.C. Their written history began when Assyrian traders (from the kingdom of Assur) arrived about 1900 B.C. and recorded business transactions on clay tablets in cuneiform. The Hittites exported copper, gold, and semiprecious stones to Assyria, and they imported woven materials from Assur and, later, horses from Babylon. A Hittite empire began to grow when King

Hattusilis I moved his capital to a strategic location. Historian O. R. Gurney explains:

> During this and the following reign the Hittite kingdom began to expand southward and eastward. This meant the emergence of the Hittite armies from behind their mountain barrier and the crossing of the formidable [mountain] range of Taurus, through which only a few passes lead. Perhaps it was the wealth of the southern plains and their ancient civilization that tempted them to this difficult operation.[32]

The Hittite armies first conquered northern Syria and then moved down the Euphrates and captured Babylon shortly after 1600 B.C. They gained military strength because they had a new weapon—the lightweight, horse-drawn chariot, invented centuries earlier in Sumer. The Hittites returned home to quell palace rebellions after capturing Babylon, but they maintained control over northern Syria.

Hittite history reveals other borrowings from Sumer. Though the Sumerian language was no longer spoken, scribes in the Hittite capital, Hattusas, studied Sumerian vigorously. Because most Sumerian words have only one syllable, Hittite scribes borrowed Sumerian cuneiform

The Hittites gradually took over the Mesopotamian region. They were heavy borrowers of Sumerian culture. At left is a lasting remnant of the Hittite capital known as the Lion Gate, dating from 1450 B.C. Below is an example of Hittite art, which resembles the art of Sumer.

words, gave them new meaning, and saved the extra time they would have taken to write the longer Akkadian or Hittite words. Tablets of Sumerian-Hittite vocabularies have been found in the capital city where learned scribes worked. Other Sumerian borrowings came directly through Syria. Cylinder-seals found in Hittite territory display subjects borrowed from the Syrians, who had borrowed them from Mesopotamia. The figure of the god standing on his animal originated in Sumer, as did the double eagle and some of the monster images. Other Hittite images as well as figures on monuments show Egyptian influence. The Hittite weather god, however, is a bearded male similar to figures from Sumer, and later monuments show that the custom of wearing a beard had spread from Sumer through Syria to the whole Hittite culture.

The Phoenicians

The Phoenicians occupied a small strip of land a hundred miles long and ten miles wide between mountains and the Mediterranean Sea. Their location forced them to become shipbuilders and traders. After being under the control first of Hammurabi and then of Egypt, they gained independence and became the main traders of the Mediterranean. For export, their artisans made objects of glass and metal, enameled vases, weapons, ornaments and jewelry, purple dye, and needlework stitched in brilliant colors. Historian Will Durant describes the extent of their trading:

> These [products their artisans made], and the exportable surplus of India and the Near East—cereals [grains], wines, textiles and precious stones— they shipped to every city of the Mediterranean far and near, bringing back, in return, lead, gold and iron from the south shores of the Black Sea, copper, cypress and corn from Cyprus, ivory from Africa, silver from Spain, tin from Britain, and slaves from everywhere. They were shrewd traders.[33]

Because Mesopotamia had no natural resources, Sumerians, especially, depended on the Phoenician sailors for metals and wood for their inventions and buildings.

Phoenician traders operated from two seaport cities, Tyre and Sidon. Their boats were low, narrow vessels about seventy feet long with a front curve that cut wind and water. One rectangular sail caught wind and helped the galley slaves, who sat in double rows on each side of the ship. Because the Phoenicians had no compasses, they traveled only by day and stayed close to shore. When their navigators learned to guide ships by the North Star, sailors ventured into the oceans and around the southern tip of Africa, two thousand years before European explorers attempted the same journey.

A drawing depicts the fleet of early Phoenicia. The Phoenicians became adept shipbuilders and sailors.

A Phoenician carving of a warrior. The man's curved beard shows Sumerian influence.

written in cuneiform were relatively heavy and took space the Phoenicians preferred to use for products. They solved the problem by developing a system of twenty-two written consonants and keeping their business records on papyrus (Egyptian paper).

Like other nations of the Ancient Near East, the Phoenicians had a belief system similar to the Sumerian religion, but the gods had different names. Each city had a Baal, or city god, who was the source of all things and ancestor of kings. The Baal of Tyre was named Melkarth. Their fertility goddess Astarte corresponds to Inanna in Sumer and Ishtar in Mari and Assur; Adoni, their dying and rising god, the consort of Astarte, corresponds to Dumuzi in Sumer and Tammuz in northern Mesopotamia. One Phoenician god had no counterpart in Sumer: Moloch was worshiped by sacrificing children as burnt offerings.

The Syrians

Besides moving products around the world, Phoenicia made two major contributions. Though no great art and literature originated in this small stretch of seacoast, Phoenicians spread art and culture wherever they went, exporting the ideas of Sumer and Egypt throughout the Mediterranean and into India. Their greatest contribution, however, was the perfection of the alphabet, which stemmed from their system of recording the details of their trading. Clay tablets

Syria, another nation between great powers, lay on the northern curve of the Fertile Crescent: Some mapmakers included Lebanon and Phoenicia as part of Syria. Two geographical factors contributed to its destiny as a nation. First, its land lacked the fertile soil and water found in river valleys, and its civilization developed more slowly for this reason, among others. Second, its location between mountains too steep to climb and a desert too hot to cross made Syria a trade route, called the Syrian Saddle.

The old city of Damascus, a city much like Babylon, was within Syrian borders. Close to Mari, northern Syria received its culture from Mesopotamia; southern Syria borrowed more often from Egypt. Both powerful nations invaded and controlled Syria at various times, keeping it always vigilant for warning signs of a new conflict.

The Canaanites

The word *Canaan* is an old word for a territory that included Philistia, Palestine, Israel, and Judah, all of which later became nations. Phoenicia is sometimes included with Canaan instead of Syria. Its territory extending to the Sinai peninsula, Canaan lay between the Arabian Desert and the Mediterranean Sea south of Syria. About 2200 B.C. Semite tribes pushed out of the Syrian desert; those who went east became Babylonians, and those who went west became Canaanites. Canaan was located at the crossroads between the Egyptian, Mesopotamian, and Hittite civilizations. Thus people from many places gathered there, interacted, and intermarried, giving Canaan a long stage of mixture. During that time, inhabitants tilled the soil or tended herds of sheep and asses. They developed a religion with more gods than other nations because many groups merged. Some gods were animistic spirits thought to reside in rocks, trees, and springs. Others, like the Sumerian gods, were gods of nature, representing storms, the sky, fertility, or water; or abstract gods of creation, justice, wisdom, and crafts. The Canaanites later developed fertility cults for the worship of Astarte and Adoni and sacrificed to Moloch and the individual gods of the different cities.

In spite of its varied mixture, Canaanite society had a distinctive character and outlook, and it produced two great religions. Historian Carroll Quigley describes the Canaanites:

> Vigorous, practical, almost crude; grasping, unesthetic, yet with powerful spiritual impulses; filled with sensual desires and crass superstitions, yet with basic intelligence the equal of any other peoples in history—such was the complex nature of these Canaanite peoples, a nature which leaves them, to this day, a constant puzzle and source of interest to students.[34]

The people who first moved into the territory of Canaan organized on the basis of blood groupings—the family and the clan, a collection of families. They developed the idea of a state when the different groups began to incorporate nonfamily members. Family loyalty remained strong, however, because the nation had no king to serve as a focal point for higher allegiance.

Other groups, called the Habiru (later Hebrews), also wandered the Canaanite hills. "Habiru" means people lacking either land or social position to get protection of blood relatives. These groups organized around a man who was isolated from his family and clan for such reasons as having killed a family member, having agreed to become a bondsman (one who offers services for hire), or having become a mercenary. In the absence of family ties, metalworkers or music makers, for example, formed social groups. The group of metalworkers called the Kenites derived their name from the biblical Cain, who slew his brother Abel. At various times, these nonfamily groups also organized for legal, religious, and political purposes.

For several reasons, it is difficult to pinpoint stages of mixture, gestation, and expansion in Canaanite society. For example, identifying elements usually typical of a rising civilization, such as a single location, a common language, or a single religion, were lacking. The major invention of Canaanite expansion is a form of economic organization called "commercial capitalism." Commercial capitalism consists of buying goods where they are abundant and cheap and selling them at higher prices where they are scarce. Two conditions made this practice work for the Canaanites. First, Canaan lay on the western edge of the Syrian Saddle and on the Mediterranean Sea at the point where land transportation ended and water transportation began. Second, at this place the demand for raw materials from Mesopotamia, especially metals, met the supply of raw materials brought in on boats from western Mediterranean areas. Canaanites became buyers and sellers. Entrepreneurs invested surplus wealth in ships, wharves, and warehouses. Others formed organizations for borrowing and lending money.

For more than five centuries, Canaanite civilization expanded: Its production increased, its population grew, and its territory expanded. But people stopped investing in the trading business and made profits their goal. When the society ceased to expand by economic means, the leaders tried to expand it by political and military means, but the plan failed to work and the society began to decline. Unrest in Palestine made conditions worse. Gradually Philistines from the west and Hebrews from the east encroached on the central area. Bloody conflicts broke out, and warriors burned and destroyed cities. Hebrews gained control over most of the territory and ruled from Jerusalem, but their kingdom divided, and foreign invaders eventually took over, ending Canaanite civilization.

The Hebrews

The Hebrews comprise a subgroup of Canaanite civilization, worthy of a separate discussion because they contributed a major religion to Western civilization. Perhaps originally a Semitic people, Hebrews, or Israelites or Jews as they were also called, certainly became a mixture. Much of what we know about their beliefs and practices comes from the Old Testament, a sacred literature that includes history, law, narrative stories, songs of praise, and proverbs and other wise sayings.

According to the book of Genesis in the Old Testament, Hebrew history begins when Abraham left Ur and traveled to Palestine, where he and his tribe began a nomadic life of herding in the region of Hebron. Scholars believe that he made his journey between 2200 and 1800 B.C. Yahweh, the Hebrew god, promised to make Abraham the father of a kingdom in the land of Canaan. Thereafter the wife of Abraham had one son, Isaac, who was the father of Jacob and Esau. The men of the next generation, Jacob's twelve sons, later became the founders of the twelve tribes of Israel.

Jacob's oldest sons, jealous of their father's favorite, Joseph, sold the young man into slavery in Egypt. With the help of Yahweh, however, Joseph rose to great prominence in the land he had entered as a slave. Indeed in later years he was able to bring his father, Jacob, along with his brothers and their families, to live in

The Hebrews contributed a major religion to Western civilization. At left, Yahweh promises Abraham descendants as numerous as the stars if he will leave Ur and go to Canaan. At bottom, Moses receives the ten commandments from Yahweh.

Egypt. After Joseph died, however, the Egyptians began to worry about the national security, fearing the impressive strength of the numerous Hebrew people in their midst. Thus the Egyptians enslaved the Israelite population, a condition that was maintained for many years.

To free the Hebrews from slavery, a man named Moses led them out of Egypt. At Mount Sinai, Moses received laws from Yahweh in the form of ten commandments written on two tablets. Here, God made another covenant with the Israelites, his favored people: If they kept his commandments, he would protect them and lead them to the land he had promised Abraham. The Israelites preserved their commandments in an ark, a portable box to house the tablets of the law. For many years, the people wandered in the desert with their herds and the ark of the covenant. When Moses died, Joshua, who

The Ten Commandments

The Old Testament book of Exodus tells of Moses returning from Mount Sinai and passing on to the Israelites the commandments Yahweh had given him. This translation of Exodus 19:25–20:17 is from The New Oxford Annotated Bible.

"So Moses went down to the people and told them.

Then God spoke all these words: I am the Lord your God, who brought you out of the land of Egypt, out of the house of slavery; you shall have no other gods before me.

You shall not make for yourself an idol, whether in the form of anything that is in heaven above, or that is on the earth beneath, or that is in the water under the earth. You shall not bow down to them or worship them; for I the Lord your God am a jealous God, punishing children for the iniquity of parents, to the third and fourth generation of those who reject me, but showing steadfast love to the thousandth generation of those who love me and keep my commandments.

You shall not make wrongful use of the name of the Lord your God, for the Lord will not acquit anyone who misuses his name.

Remember the sabbath day, and keep it holy. Six days you shall labor and do all your work. But the seventh day is a sabbath to the Lord your God; you shall not do any work—you, your son or your daughter, your male or female slave, your livestock, or the alien resident in your towns. For in six days the Lord made the heaven and earth, the sea, and all that is in them, but rested the seventh day; therefore the Lord blessed the sabbath day and consecrated it.

Honor your father and your mother, so that your days may be long in the land that the Lord your God is giving you.

You shall not murder.

You shall not commit adultery.

You shall not steal.

You shall not bear false witness against your neighbor.

You shall not covet your neighbor's house; you shall not covet your neighbor's wife, or male or female slave, or ox, or anything that belongs to your neighbor."

succeeded the aged prophet as leader of the Hebrews, began military campaigns to establish the promised kingdom.

Under Joshua, and for many generations after his death, the Hebrew tribes maintained a loose confederacy, capturing, losing, and recapturing lands of the Canaanites and other neighbors. Near the end of the second millennium, the people, dissatisfied with a new generation of hereditary religious leaders, requested a king, "like the other nations."

Saul, a member of the tribe of Benjamin, was anointed the first king. In 1000 B.C. the second king, David, began a royal dynasty that lasted many generations.

David was succeeded by his son Solomon, who acquired great wealth and built a temple and a palace in Jerusalem. After Solomon's death, the kingdom split into two parts: Israel in the north and Judah in the south. Israel was conquered by the Assyrians in 722 B.C., and when Judah fell to the Babylonians in 586 B.C. the Hebrew nation ceased to occupy its traditional land.

How does this biblical story mesh with the history of the Ancient Near East? If Abraham was indeed a real person who came out of Ur, he likely left during the Third Dynasty, after the construction of Ur-Nammu's ziggurat with its hanging gardens. In Palestine, secular historians say,

An artist's conception of the great temple of Solomon in Jerusalem. Solomon's reign marked Judah's golden age.

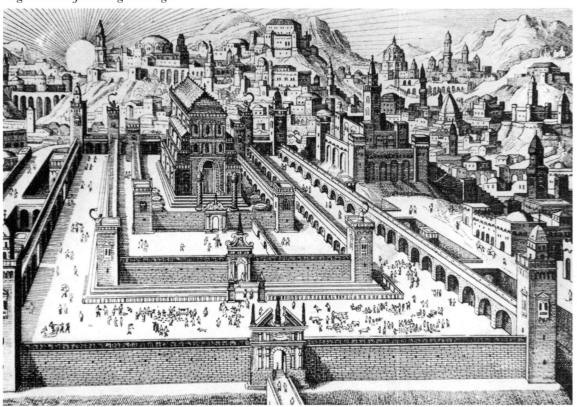

Abraham's people were Habiru tribes banded together under the protection of Yahu, a minor Canaanite god. Some of these Habiru tribes worked in copper mines in Sinai; others went to Egypt, where their numbers grew. Because Egyptian rule was oppressive, the Hebrews complained. Moses received a message from Yahweh (formerly Yahu) to obtain the permission of the pharaoh, the Egyptian ruler, to lead the Hebrews out of Egypt. When this had been accomplished, Moses led the Hebrews east to the Sinai Desert rather than following the regular roads to Canaan.

Hebrews in Canaan established an agricultural life similar to that of pastoral Sumer. They had no river to overflow, but Palestine had abundant spring rains, making it "a land flowing with milk and honey," in accordance with a statement in the Old Testament (Exodus 3:17). Historian Will Durant describes how the Hebrews developed agriculture:

> In ancient days the spring rains that fed the land were stored in cisterns or brought back to the surface by multitudes of wells, and distributed over the country by a network of canals; this was the physical basis of Jewish civilization. The soil, so nourished, produced barley, wheat and corn, the vine throve on it, and trees bore olives, figs, dates or other fruits on every slope. When war came and devastated these artificially fertile fields, or when some conqueror exiled to distant regions the families that had cared for them, the desert crept in eagerly, and in a few years undid the work of generations.[35]

Wars disrupted this successful farm life when tribal villages fought, since the men had to leave their fields and herds to be soldiers. Many bloody conflicts occurred before the twelve Hebrew tribes had conquered the necessary Canaanite cities and organized first into a confederacy and then into a nation under a king.

The Hebrew nation lasted 450 years. Led by Joshua, the tribes captured the territory as far east as the walled city of Jericho, one of the oldest cities in the Middle East. Later, King David expanded the national boundaries, began to accumulate wealth, and made Jerusalem the capital. Under Solomon, one of David's sons and his designated successor, the nation reached its peak.

Like the Canaanites, the Hebrews acquired wealth by commercial capitalism. They were middlemen in trade between Arabs near the Red Sea and Canaanites near the Phoenician coast. Solomon built a greater port city, Ezion-Geber, and controlled overland trade routes. He became very rich bringing Indian spices, myrrh, incense, gold, silver, ivory, apes, and peacocks to the Arabs and copper, tin, and iron to cities in Canaan. On other overland routes, he brought iron and copper from the Jordan Valley and horses bred at Megiddo. With his wealth, he took many wives and lived in luxury. Using cedar trees from Lebanon, he built a grand palace for himself and a temple for the ark of the covenant.

Religious Differences

Little distinguished the Hebrews from the Canaanites except in the matter of religion. The entire Ancient Near East had adopted the religion of Sumer with a few variations in practice and different names for gods. The Hebrews focused on a single god, Yahweh, but it took centuries to put monotheism (the exclusive worship of one god) into practice. Yahweh, the god of Moses, was a merciful god whose laws addressed two kinds of behavior, as set forth in the Ten Commandments. The first three instruct the people to worship no other gods and to treat Yahweh's name with respect; the other seven set out rules for acting decently in dealing with people, to ensure harmonious relations among the members of family and tribe. The Hebrews had the usual human trouble treating one another decently, but they had particular trouble putting aside all traces of the old fertility religion. As members of the broader agricultural community, they were surrounded by people who maintained allegiance to the fertility cult. Many Hebrews feared that unless they performed the ancient rituals, their crops might die.

The Hebrew nation failed as others had failed when leaders accumulated wealth for their luxury and stopped investing in inventions. Solomon overworked and overtaxed the ordinary people until they were tired and poor. When the next ruler, Rehoboam, promised to be even harsher than his father, Solomon, had been, all the tribes except one seceded from the kingdom. Divided into two parts, Israel and Judah, which were further racked by problems of many descriptions, the nation was too weak to withstand outside invasion. Each part fell to foreign conquerors, who took Hebrews away as slaves. During the exile, Judean scholars and scribes collected many of the people's traditional stories and wrote much of what is now called the Old Testament to record national history and preserve Hebrew thought. After the exile, the Hebrews formulated Judaism, the religion practiced by Jews to this day. Out of Judaism developed Christianity. Canaan produced these two major religions.

The Aramaeans

Between the fourteenth and twelfth centuries B.C., a Semitic people, the Aramaeans, entered the Fertile Crescent, not far from the caravan routes between Babylonia and the Mediterranean ports. The Aramaeans owned camels, mules, and donkeys, which they used to haul goods all over the Ancient Near East. They had a reputation as crude wanderers who contributed nothing to the civilization except large numbers of people. Yet they were excellent scribes and businessmen who, like the Phoenician traders, needed an efficient way to keep records. They adopted the Phoenician alphabet and introduced the script wherever they hauled goods. By 500 B.C. their language, Aramaic, had become the lingua franca (the common language of business used by people of different languages) in the whole area. Aramaic even replaced Hebrew. Though most of the Old Testament was written in Hebrew, some of it was in Aramaic. Some Christian communities in northern Iraq still speak Aramaic, which was the language used by Jesus. Few languages today have such a long continuous history.

Chapter

7 Universal Empire: The Assyrians, 1600–609 B.C.

In the evolution of civilizations, the stage of conflict sometimes lasts a long time, but eventually one nation gains control over the central core of nations and goes on to subjugate the peripheral states to create a universal empire. After Hammurabi unified the nation, the name Babylonia replaced the name Mesopotamia for the area extending from north of Assur to the Persian Gulf. For centuries, one nation after another fought for control of Babylonia. Except for a few dynasties and individual kings, the history of the period is a series of one war campaign after another during which the same things happened: cities were destroyed and warriors were slaughtered. Following conquest, the victors demanded tributes from the defeated, to gain wealth necessary to launch more elaborate war campaigns. Finally, Assyria gained control of Babylonia and all the nations to Egypt's border and part of Egypt.

Although Hammurabi's son and grandson carried on the Babylonian dynasty when the old leader died, discontent had already set in. Taking advantage of a growing trend, the administrators in Ur started a local insurrection. To punish them and to show his power, Hammurabi's son Samsu-iluna (1749–1712 B.C.) demolished the walls of Ur and burned the city—the common people's homes and the beautiful buildings built by Ur-Nammu and his son. This attack represented only one of the city's many destructions, but this time the inhabitants were too demoralized and poor to face yet another rebuilding. Samsu-iluna had, however, saved thousands of Sumerian tablets, which he had scribes rewrite into the Babylonian language. Though Sumerian

A Hittite warrior. Hammurabi's three-hundred-year dynasty crumbled after the Hittites sacked Babylon in 1595 B.C.

The Burning of Ur

In this excerpt from Excavations at Ur, *Sir Leonard Woolley describes the devastation caused by Samsu-iluna's attack in 1737 B.C.*

"The ruins bear eloquent testimony to the thoroughness of that destruction. The fortifications were dismantled—this indeed one might expect; every temple that we found had been plundered, cast down and burned; every house had been consumed with fire; the whole of the great city ceased to exist. In the houses it often happened that where walls were not left standing very high we could note lying over the tips of them horizontal strata of dust and sand and ashes, sure proof that for some length of time the ruins had been undisturbed, long enough for the gradual processes of wind and rain to fill in the hollows and thereafter start the ordered burial of the dead town. Of course people did come back to what had been their home, but they had neither the morale nor the means to rebuild it. Where the house walls were still standing fairly high they would squat in the ruins, patching the broken walls with old bricks, stamping a new mud floor over the wreckage that filled the old rooms, but would content themselves with the one story which meant less work and less materials."

was still used for religious purposes, it was thereafter a dead language. Kings of Babylon of Hammurabi's dynasty reigned over a still-prosperous but dwindling empire for another century. The three-hundred-year dynasty ended in 1595 B.C. when the Hittites invaded it, sacked it, and plundered the statues of its gods, including Marduk.

Following the Hittite invasion, historical records are unclear. Gulkishar, a Sealand king from the area just north of the Persian Gulf, seems to have established a dynasty that may have ruled the south and controlled Babylon for a century. A tablet remaining from the "year he became king" gives procedures for the manufacture of two types of red glass. These are the earliest known instructions for glass making, though references to glass go back to the Third Dynasty of Ur. Records show that Gulkishar held off Kassite invasions for a while, but the Kassites eventually prevailed and established an empire.

The Kassites

The Kassites, who ruled for about four hundred years, had for centuries lived in the central region of the Zagros Mountains, unconcerned about the events in the Tigris–Euphrates valley. The arrival of aggressive Indo-Europeans in their area stimulated the Kassites to learn how to be warriors and how to raise horses, and then Kassite farmers began moving into the valley in small groups and settling. At some point around 1500 B.C. Kassite soldiers took control of Babylon. Because tablets that may tell their history are yet to be translated, the early kings are mostly unknown. Archaeologist Leonard Woolley says of the Kassites:

> Good fighting men they must have been, to achieve their position, but they seem not to have known how to use it. The early Kassite period is a blank page in the history of Mesopotamia; politically the kings were insignificant, the arts stagnated, no great buildings gave lustre to the names of the rulers and no records were kept of their uneventful rule.[36]

Perhaps the Kassites contributed little that was new because they adopted the Babylonian language and the age-old traditions begun by the Sumerians, thus saving Mesopotamian culture from oblivion. The Kassites reinstated Marduk as god; passed down scientific work, medical and astronomical observations, and myths and legends; and preserved religion and philosophy. As their empire expanded, they spread the culture from Anatolia to Egypt. One king, Kuri-galzu II, stood out. As a ruler about 1400 B.C., he restored Ur and built a new town called Aqar Quf. Excavators found there a ziggurat built in the style of those in Sumer dedicated to the deities Enlil, Ninlil, and their son Ninurta. Archaeologist Georges Roux says: "The presence of these Sumerian gods in a city founded by a Kassite king proved the degree to which the foreigners had been assimilated."[37]

Kassite Invention

The Kassites did make small contributions. They found a new way to measure fields by using boundary stones, and they initiated a system of showing ownership by recording the transactions through which people received land. They invented a dating system for years—"first," "second," and so on—and left a few small monuments. Sometimes incorrectly given credit for domesticating horses, the Kassites were, however, responsible for making the use of horses as draft animals more common. Excavations north of Babylon at Nuzi provide evidence of Kassite invention and trade. Excavators uncovered a palace with an elaborate drainage system and a toilet that flushed with water from above. At the same site they found pottery with white designs on black, a kind of ceramic ware often associated with Syria.

During Kassite reign, other Near Eastern countries were fighting one another. Either too weak or too smart to join the wars, the Kassites ruled over a peaceful land. After 1480 B.C., the whole area to the west "went up in flames."[38] Egypt had been invaded and had recovered. Then its army took Lebanon and Syria from the Hittites; then the Hittites took Syria back. Ramses II decided to take all the territory to the Euphrates, but the Egyptian monarch found the Hittites stronger than he had thought. In the famous battle of Qadesh in 1285 B.C., neither side decisively defeated the other. Both parties claimed victory, however, and they signed a peace treaty sixteen years later. By this time, Assyrians, who were waging war in the northern mountains and positioning themselves at Assur, threatened the Hittite-Egyptian alliance.

Defeat of the Kassites

In the southeast the Elamites began warring, reoccupied Susa, and attacked Babylon, as did the Assyrians. But it was the

Marduk, Babylon's patron god, was taken into captivity by the Elamites and recaptured by Nebuchadrezzar I.

Elamites who brought an end to the Kassite empire. They carried Babylonian art treasures back to Elam and took the statue of Marduk into captivity. Thus, a long but obscure empire ended in 1171 B.C. By that time Mesopotamian culture had been adopted throughout the Ancient Near East. "Gilgamesh" had been translated into Hittite, and copies of Babylonian legends could be found on the banks of the Nile in Egypt.

The post-Kassite period in Babylon was unstable, ruled by six dynasties of local kings who were unable to match Assyrian warriors determined to make Assyria supreme. The first Nebuchadrezzar (1126–1105 B.C.) was the most important because he avenged the Elamites for ending the Kassite empire. Nebuchadrezzar I led his troops on a surprise march in the hottest part of the summer. Joan Oates quotes from an inscription describing the march:

> "The axes in the soldiers' hands burnt like fire and the road-surfaces scorched like flame. In the wells there was no water . . . the strength of the powerful horses gave out, and the legs of even the strongest warrior weakened." According to the same inscription "the face of the sun was darkened by the clouds of dust" raised by the battle. Nonetheless Nebuchadrezzar was victorious.[39]

The victory recovered the statue of Marduk, the god who was now restored as the supreme god of Babylon. In the minds of Babylonians, the god's statue had to be present for the city to receive Marduk's protection.

For the next three centuries, the Chaldaeans, the Aramaeans, and the Assyrians fought to control Babylon. The Chaldaeans, who lived around the swamps and lakes near the Persian Gulf, had date farms, as well as herds of cattle and horses. They began a dynasty when Assyria was weak and achieved control over the southern trade routes. One king, Nabonassar, established the Chaldaeans as astronomers because he kept diaries recording the movements of the stars, the river levels, and the day-to-day changes in the weather. The Aramaeans were tribal people from northern Syria who settled in Babylonian towns and villages and made raids on cities. Their language, the Semitic dialect called Aramaic, gradually had replaced Akkadian as the spoken language in the former kingdom of Babylonia. Moreover, it was the first Mesopotamian language to be written in cursive alphabetic script, not in cuneiform characters.

The Rise of Assyria

Of the three competing powers, the Assyrians took and retook Babylon and established a universal empire, Quigley's fifth stage in the life cycle of a civilization. Assyria got its name from Assur, an old city-state once ruled by the kings of Ur and later an independent kingdom extending to Nineveh. At the end of the tenth century, Assyria was at a low point. Its territory was only a hundred miles long and fifty miles wide, but it had an army and, perhaps most important, weak neighbors. Assyrians fought first to defend themselves and second to fulfill their king's destiny to stand above other kings as they believed their god Assur stood above other gods.

By 910 B.C., the Assyrians reestablished dominance in Babylon. Between 884 and 860 B.C., they conquered the Aramaeans, reconquered Babylon, and controlled Syria all the way to the Mediterranean. In 722 B.C., their goal was complete mastery of the Fertile Crescent by 700 B.C. They accomplished this aim by deploying trained soldiers under a string of good leaders, by the systematic use of terrorization, and by good political administration.

Assyrian peasants were highly trained and efficient soldiers. Equipped with iron striking weapons and bows with iron-tipped arrows, they fought on horseback and in chariots. Leaders inspired them by giving feasts and celebrations after victories, providing food and drink for the people as well as the soldiers. They paraded prisoners and boasted about the warriors they had tortured and killed. Joan Oates quotes a war leader's description of an attack on Babylon, recorded in the Assyrian royal annals; it is typical of the blood-thirsty tactics of the Assyrians:

> 13,000 of their warriors I cut down with the sword. Their blood like the waters of a stream I caused to run through the squares of their city. The corpses of their soldiers I piled in heaps. . . . His [the Babylonian king's] royal bed, his royal couch, the treasure of his palaces, his property, his gods and everything from his palace, without number, I carried away. His captive warriors were given to the soldiers of my land like grasshoppers. The city I destroyed, I devastated, I burned with fire.[40]

Other records show that the Assyrian soldiers decapitated wounded enemy troops and brought the heads back to camp or

Assyrians count the severed heads of conquered enemy soldiers. Assyria had an efficient and well-trained army that was bent on conquest.

hung them in trees. They took cattle and sheep, and they burned captives and children.

The kings used three successful practices to administer their territory. First, they developed a close-knit empire in which nations that had warred began to trade and interact peacefully; with the core region at peace, armies could attack distant neighbors. Second, they forced conquered people to leave their homeland and dispersed them in other societies. Conquered people brought their inventions and customs, and the exchange with local residents gave new energy to the nation. Third, they coordinated the empire by improving the oversight capabilities of governors assigned to rule conquered cities. This entailed building a network of roads and wide highways and setting up a relay system of messengers to deliver messages quickly—the first postal system. Assyria's universal empire was built by a series of ruthless kings. Among the more important ones were Ashurnasirpal, Tiglath-pileser, Sargon II, Sennacherib, and Ashurbanipal.

Five Important Assyrian Kings

Ashurnasirpal II, the first great Assyrian monarch who reigned from 883 to 859 B.C., quelled local rebellions and paved the way for later kings. When he heard that a southern city was about to rebel, Ashurnasirpal took an army two hundred miles in the heat of summer to put down the rebellion. When he had conquered the local cities, he started toward Syria and the Mediterranean, advancing about twenty miles a day, cutting a cruel path as he went. At the Mediterranean, he washed his weapons in the sea and sacrificed to

Ashurnasirpal II was the first great Assyrian monarch who reigned from 883 to 859 B.C. He paved the way for later conquerors.

the gods. As tribute he took gold, silver, tin, copper, linen, monkeys, and ivory. On his return to Assyria, he took Hittite and Aramaean kingdoms in northern Syria. On an inscription, Ashurnasirpal II described his methods of warfare, here quoted by historian Carroll Quigley:

> In the midst of the mighty mountain I slaughtered them, and, with their blood, dyed the mountain red like wool. . . . I carried off their spoil and their possessions. The heads of the warriors I cut off, and I formed them into a pillar over against the city. . . . I flayed all the chief men who had revolted and I covered the pillar with their skins; some I walled up within the pillar; some I impaled upon the pillar on stakes. . . . Many within the border of my own land I flayed, and I spread their skins upon the walls, and I cut off the limbs of the royal officers who had rebelled.[41]

Despite his cruelty, Ashurnasirpal II, who was also a skilled hunter, had redeeming qualities. Because he liked botany and zoology, he brought back beasts, trees, and seeds for his nation. And he built himself a palace in Kalhu, the city that is Nimrud in modern Iraq.

If Ashurnasirpal paved the way for kings who followed, Tiglath-pileser III, who reigned from 744 to 727 B.C., was the founder of the Assyrian Empire. He instituted the reforms that gave Assyria internal peace. He reorganized the army and established a modern communication system with special runners who carried reports and letters. He enforced the law and the payment of tributes. To cut down on revolt, he moved whole towns to new territories. Village men walked with soldiers, and women and children rode in carts. These sad-faced people were uprooted from their land and homes and given small plots of land in a new place. Tiglath-pileser III expanded the territory by taking towns east in the Zagros Mountains to Tepe Giyan and west to Tyre and Sidon on the Mediterranean, annexing half of Israel on the way. After taking Babylon, he became king there in 728, but died a year later.

After the short, uneventful reign of the son of Tiglath-pileser III, the next ruler, Sargon II, almost secured the empire against rebellions and did expand its territory. Because Tiglath-pileser III had cut off trade routes to Egypt and Elam, neither nation could attack Assyria. In-stead, both countries fostered rebellions in Assyrian vassals. A vassal is a conquered city or nation administered by a governor appointed by the victorious king. For example, Egypt staged two uprisings in Syria, but Sargon II put down both. In 714 B.C., Sargon II launched a successful, large-scale campaign. By 710, Assyria held all of Syria-Palestine except Judah, most of the Zagros range, Media and Urartu or Ararat (near the border between Turkey and Iran). The Egyptians were friendly, the Elamites and Phrygians (western Turkey) peaceful. Babylon had gone back to Chaldaean rule, but the Assyrian king retook it. The reign of Sargon II lasted from 721 to 705 B.C.; at the end of it, the Assyrian Empire was larger and stronger than ever.

(Left) A carved wall panel shows Ashurnasirpal and his cupbearer. Sargon II (right) strengthened and enlarged the empire by conquering societies that were hostile to the Assyrians and improving relations with those that were peaceful.

Sargon II also had great wealth acquired from tributes paid by many vassals. After ruling in the early days from Ashurnasirpal's palace at Kalhu, Sargon II built his own palace in his own town near the modern village of Khorsabad. Sargon's fortress, as it was called, stood on a fifty-foot-high platform; it had over two hundred rooms, thirty courtyards, and a seven-story ziggurat. The royal palace had fine art to decorate it: huge bull-man statues guarding the door, blue-glazed bricks painted with divine symbols, frescoes (art painted on fresh plaster), and a mile and a half of relief carvings. Since the whole city was built in ten years, thousands of prisoners of war and hundreds of artists and artisans must have worked on it. Although in a display inscription Sargon had asked the god Assur to grant him a long and healthy life, he died two years later in battle. His successors preferred to rule from Nineveh, and the Khorsabad palace fell into ruin.

Sargon's son Sennacherib (reigned 704–681 B.C.) followed his father as king. He spent the first part of his reign putting down the revolts of the Elamites, the Aramaeans, and many others. The king of Judah, called Hezekiah in the Bible and Ezekiah by some historians, cut ties with Nineveh, and Sennacherib went to attack. When the Assyrian army reached Jerusalem, three of Ezekiah's officials met three representatives of Sennacherib. The Assyrians promised two thousand horses if the Jews would open Jerusalem's gates. Ezekiah refused, but a compromise was reached: the Assyrians would withdraw, sparing the city, upon payment of staggering amounts of gold and silver. In addition, Ezekiah's daughters, his harem, his male and female musicians, and several

Sennacherib became king after the death of his father, Sargon II. Sennacherib was killed by his own son for destroying Babylon.

cities were to be turned over to the Philistines, traditional enemies of the Hebrew people. Sennacherib planned to end his campaign by invading Egypt, but thousands of his soldiers died mysteriously on the way. According to the Old Testament, the angel of the Lord "smote" them; other sources say a plague of rats or a pestilence ravaged the Assyrian troops.

Six years later, Sennacherib planned a sea and land campaign to expand Assyrian territory to the Persian Gulf. He sent a fleet of ships down the Tigris River from Nineveh. Because the mouth of the Tigris was too swampy for navigation, he had an army of slaves carry the ships to the Euphrates River, at the place where the two rivers run closest. Meanwhile, the land army continued its march. The campaign succeeded, but it set off a round of battles with the Elamites. Sennacherib nearly lost

Letter to a King

In Letters from Mesopotamia, *historian A. Leo Oppenheim translates a letter to Assurbanipal [Ashurbanipal] from one of his technical advisers. The letter concerns an eclipse.*

"To my lord, the king of all countries (Assurbanipal), from your servant Bēl-u[. . .]:

May the gods, Bēl, Nabû, and Šamas bless Your Majesty.

If an eclipse occurs, but it is not observed in the capital, such an eclipse is considered not to have occurred. 'The capital' means the city in which the king happens to be staying. Now, there were clouds everywhere; we thus do not know whether the eclipse did or did not occur. The lord of all kings should write to Assur and to all cities such as Babylon, Nippur, Uruk, and Borsippa. Possibly it was observed in these cities. The king should also watch out for the regular reports . . . [*break*] I have already written everything to Your Majesty concerning the portent of an eclipse that occurred in the months Addaru and Nisannu. And as to the apotropaic [intended to ward off evil] rites for the eclipse which they have already performed, what harm can be done (even if the eclipse did not take place)? It is advantageous to perform the rites; the king should therefore not send (the experts) away.

The great gods who live in the city of Your Majesty have covered the sky and have thus not shown the eclipse. This is what the king should know: to wit, that this eclipse has no relation to Your Majesty or his country. On this account the king should be happy.

PS: If the storm god Adad thunders in the month of Nisannu (it means) the 'small barley' crop will diminish."

---

one battle, and the defeat enraged him so much that he avenged himself on the sacred city of Babylon. Archaeologist Georges Roux quotes the Assyrian tyrant:

As a hurricane proceeds, I attacked it and, like a storm, I overthrew it. . . . Its inhabitants, young and old, I did not spare and with their corpses I filled the streets of the city. . . . The town itself and its houses, from their foundations to their roofs I devastated, I destroyed, by fire I overthrew. . . . In order that, in future, even the soil of its temples be forgotten, by water I ravaged it, I turned it into pastures.[42]

For this crime, one of Sennacherib's own sons smashed him to death with statues as he prayed in a temple. To this day, in towns near the Turkey-Iraq border, rocks carved with gigantic images of Senacherib standing before the gods still exist for tourists to see.

Ashurbanipal ruled over the Assyrian Empire from 668 to 631 B.C., when it was at its largest but was starting to weaken.

Esarhaddon, the father of Ashurbanipal, had subdued Egypt, taken the southern part, and installed governors, but Assyrian control lasted only two years. The Egyptians kept revolting, and Ashurbanipal kept putting them down. By the middle of his reign, however, the Assyrians had been expelled from Egypt. There were also battles in Phoenicia in the north, and Ashurbanipal had continued Sennacherib's war with the Elamites, destroying the whole country. After the sack of the Elamite city of Susa, Ashurbanipal celebrated his

An Assyrian relief depicts Ashurbanipal feasting with his queen in the royal garden. Ashurbanipal ruled over the Assyrian Empire as it was beginning to decline in influence and power.

victory by harnessing three Elamite princes and an Arabian king to his chariot. At that time, the Assyrian Empire looked strong, but the soldiers were weary after years of bloody wars, Egypt was lost, Elam and Babylon were ruined, and the Phoenicians were enslaved. After 639 B.C., the records of Ashurbanipal come to a stop, leaving the last eight years of his reign unknown.

The Fall and Legacy of the Assyrian Empire

After Ashurbanipal died in 631 B.C., internal troubles broke out, and the empire declined and failed. Babylonia became independent and in 626 B.C. established its eleventh and last dynasty, called the Chaldaean Dynasty. The same year saw the beginning of the Babylonian chronicles, records similar to the Assyrian annals. By 615 B.C., all of Sumer and Akkad had been liberated, and the Medes had invaded Assyria and marched to Nineveh. By the end of 612 B.C., Assyria's enemies had destroyed its three main cities: Assur, the religious hub; Nineveh, the administrative center; and Nimrud, the military headquarters. The universal kingdom that had ruled for three centuries lasted for only three years after its cities had fallen into heaps and ruins. Historians T. Walter Wallbank and Alastair M. Taylor write that the end was bound to come: "The Assyrian empire obtained its main resources from booty and conquest. The failure of such a system was inevitable in the long run."[43]

In spite of its unending attention to war, the Assyrian Empire did leave a legacy. Its artists and builders primarily adopted Sumerian forms, but they developed a few new features. All three of the main Assyrian cities had imperial arsenals, a type of facility not found in Sumer. Assyrians needed large, secure compounds to store and maintain their war equipment. The arsenal at Nimrud had a central parade ground with a throne at one end, where the king sat to review the troops as part of the New Year festival. In addition, the arsenal kept stables for the stallions and mules, storage areas for equipment and weapons, repair shops, food storage areas, and warehouse for the goods looted in foreign lands. The arsenals had no outstanding architectural features but their size.

In Assyria, temple architecture was less important than palace architecture. Palaces were big and grand, decorated with murals and relief carvings, statues and stone carvings. Because large quarries of the white material were available nearby, alabaster sculptures adorned the entrances.

Huge sculptures of winged and human-headed bulls or lions stood at doorways to protect the entrance to the king's palace, and steles commemorated kings' accomplishments. A black obelisk now in the British Museum in London, portrays a king receiving tributes from a defeated subject and bears inscriptions of the king's victories. Most internal palace decorations portray single scenes of kings and their courtiers in huge figures. For example, in Tiglath-pileser's palace, murals show the monarch in military campaigns or hunting scenes, painted in red, blue, and black on white plaster. A relief carving from Sennacherib's palace depicts the transport of a sculpture from a quarry in the wooded

A Royal Banquet

In The Ancient Near East: A New Anthology of Texts and Pictures, *editor James B. Pritchard includes an inscription entitled "The Banquet of Ashurnasirpal II." The excerpt quoted here gives the food list.*

"When Ashurnasirpal, king of Assyria, inaugurated the palace in Calah [Kalhu], a palace of joy and (erected with) great ingenuity, he invited into it Ashur, the great lord and the gods of his entire country, (he prepared a banquet of) 1,000 fatted head of cattle, 1,000 calves, *10,000* stable sheep, 15,000 lambs—for my lady Ishtar (alone) 200 head of cattle (and) 1,000 *siḫḫu*-sheep—1,000 spring lambs, 500 stags, 500 gazelles, 1,000 ducks, 500 geese, 500 *kurkû*-geese, 1,000 *mesuku*-birds, 1,000 *qāribu*-birds, 10,000 doves, 10,000 *sukanūnu*-doves, 10,000 other (assorted) small birds, 10,000 (assorted) fish, 10,000 jerboa [rodents that lived in the region at the time], 10,000 (assorted) eggs; 10,000 loaves of bread, 10,000 (jars of) beer, 10,000 skins with wine, 10,000 pointed bottom vessels with *sŭ'u*-seeds in sesame oil, 100,000 small pots with *ṣarhu*-condiment, 1,000 wooden crates with vegetables, 300 (containers with) oil, 300 (containers with) salted *seeds*, 300 (containers with) mixed *raqqūte*-plants, 100 with *kudimmu*-spice . . . , 100 (containers with) parched barley, 100 (containers with) green *abahšinnu*-stalks, 100 (containers with) fine mixed beer, 100 pomergranates, 100 bunches of grapes, 100 mixed *zamru*-fruits, 100 pistachio cones, 100 with the fruits of *šūši*-tree, 100 with garlic, 100 with onions, 100 with *kuniphu* (seeds), 100 with . . . turnips, 100 with *ḫinḫinnu*-spice, 100 with *budû*-spice, 100 with honey, 100 with rendered butter, 100 with roasted . . . barley, 100 with roasted *sŭ'u*-seeds, 100 with *karkartu*-plants, 100 with fruits of the *ti'atu*-tree, 100 with *kasû*-plants, 100 with milk, 100 with cheese. . . .

When I inaugurated the palace at Calah I treated for ten days with food and drink 47,074 persons, men and women, who were bid to come from across my entire country."

The Assyrians were fond of sculptures, especially those depicting kings' accomplishments. Here, Ashurbanipal hunts lions (left). After the kill, he pours libations to the gods over the lions' corpses (below).

countryside with horses and slaves pulling the raft. A famous carving in Ashurbanipal's palace shows the king hunting lions in the top register and pouring libations over the kill on the bottom.

New in Assyria were the ivories. Artists made relief carvings on ivory plaques to be used on furniture and panels or in the round; they did fine detailed works of human figures, animals, trees, and warriors.

Assyrian Libraries

In Sennacherib's palace archaeologists uncovered two libraries with twenty-five thousand tablets. Some of them record letters, contracts, and inscriptions of the king's economic and historical accomplishments. Others record literary, religious, and scientific compositions. Both kings and scribes deserve credit for the fine quality of these cuneiform tablets. In a well, archaeologists found the first book with "pages." Inscribed in cuneiform on ivory covered with wax and placed in a wood frame with gold hinges, fifteen panels open accordion style, like a Japanese screen. The cover bears Sargon II's name and title, plus a note that the book should be kept in the Khorsabad palace.

Tablets from the libraries pass down information about Assyrian medicine, which was considered an art, not a science, and Assyrian pharmacy. The belief prevailed that disease was punishment from the gods for human sins. The physicians' art consisted in part of recognizing the hands of various gods in patients' symptoms. Demons, too, were thought to possess sick people or parts of the body. Since disease was believed to reflect moral illness, magical or religious cures, such as incantation, sacrifice, or exorcism, were sometimes used. Yet for all their reliance on beliefs that are now considered to be unscientific, ancient Assyrian physicians also pinpointed natural factors, such as dirt, bad food and drinks, and contagion as causes of illness. Pharmacists prepared ointments, inhalants, and lotions as cures. For example, difficulty in breathing might be treated with a paste made of sheep kidney, dates, fir turpentine, pine turpentine, laurel, resin of galbanum, mustard seeds, and cantharis. The ingredients were to be ground and placed on a piece of gazelle's skin and applied to the patient, who was to wear the paste, called a poultice, for three days. During that time, the patient was to drink sweet beer, take very hot food, and stay in a warm place.

Tablets from the libraries also pass down Assyrian science and mathematics. Science, including social science, is usually comprised of lists—lists of plants, animals, minerals, places, medical prescriptions, astronomical observations, and celebrations. Assyrians and Babylonians certainly knew more about science than the lists tell. To

This depiction of an Assyrian palace shows the Assyrians in their heyday. Palace construction was more important to the Assyrians than temple construction.

make aqueducts and to transport and set up huge blocks of stone required knowledge of physics; to make paint pigments, colored glass, and enameled bricks required knowledge of chemistry. Two kinds of mathematical information appear on the tablets: lists and problems. Scribes made lists of numbers arranged in various increasing or decreasing series and tables of multiplication and division.

Algebra was more advanced than geometry. Students learned all of their subjects without textbooks. Perhaps the lists and the problems gave students both information and an opportunity to practice writing.

The Assyrian universal empire may have appeared peaceful from the outside, but keeping peace entailed constant conflict with discontented rebels. With so great a proportion of the empire's wealth centralized in the king's capital cities, the vassals had less and less. Georges Roux said this of the advancing decay:

> The Assyrians took much and gave very little, with the result that if the state was rich, its distant subjects were destitute and in almost constant rebellion. The system upon which the empire was founded had in itself the germs of its own destruction.[44]

8 Decay: The End of Ur and Babylon, 609–331 B.C.

When civilizations rise and fall, all the stages of their development overlap. During the Third Dynasty of Ur when kings began to emphasize wealth and warfare, decline and decay set in. During the long period of conflict when city-states fought to control the whole Tigris-Euphrates valley, warfare continued to take the kings' attention, a focus that moved the civilization further toward decay. Then the Assyrian kings spent three centuries centralizing wealth, dominating others with cruel wars, and neglecting investment in both inventions and the arts. The masses of people, impoverished by taxes and demoralized by the destruction of their cities, lived without hope, as illustrated by the reaction when Ur was burned. The period of decay was long and slow, but efforts to rebuild were still alive in Babylon.

Several powers fought to gain territory and dominate the region once held by the Assyrians. One nation, however, took action to restore the Tigris-Euphrates valley and keep the ancient traditions alive. Babylonia, because of its location and the determination of its Chaldaean rulers, became the nation to restore the Sumerian-Akkadian traditions and cities. The neo-Babylonian kings devoted time and money to rebuilding sanctuaries, reviving temple rituals, and celebrating religious festivals, and they spent less time and money on war. Reconstruction began in the main cities from Sippar to Uruk to Ur.

Nebuchadrezzar II, who came to power in 604 B.C., was the ruler who did the most to make the new or Neo-Babylonian Empire successful. First, he drove the Egyptians out of Syria, eliminating the chance for them to develop another universal empire, and secured the trade routes necessary for Babylon's prosperity. Then he put down rebellions in Syria, Palestine, and coastal towns, where people hated to be paying tributes again after the Assyrians had taxed them heavily. The king of Judah, however, refused to accept his aides' advice to pay Nebuchadrezzar's requested tax. As a result, in 597 B.C., Nebuchadrezzar attacked Judah's capital, Jerusalem, deported three thousand Hebrews to Babylon, and laid an eighteen-month siege around the city. King Zedekiah finally escaped from Jerusalem and fled to Jericho. Then in 586 B.C. Nebuchadrezzar's forces broke down the walls of Jerusalem, looted the city, and burned the beautiful temple King Solomon had built. Then they captured Zedekiah, forced him to witness the execution of his three sons, poked out his eyes, and took the blinded man to Babylon. Though some of the Hebrews escaped to Egypt, thousands more were taken as prisoners to Babylon. This was a devastating experience for the Hebrew people, who believed that the land from which Nebuchadrezzar removed them had been theirs by virtue of the covenant between Abraham and Yahweh.

At home Nebuchadrezzar ordered the rebuilding of old Sumerian cities and the reconstruction of public buildings in Babylon. He made Babylon a spectacular city, more splendid than any in the Ancient Near East. By the standards of the day, Babylon became a great metropolis. Covering five hundred acres, it had a population of a hundred thousand people and over a thousand temples. Special attention went to rebuilding its walls, its streets and gates, its palace, and its ziggurat.

To fortify Babylon, Nebuchadrezzar had the city surrounded by an inner and an outer wall. Built of burned bricks, the double inner wall had nine gates, each topped by a high tower and a chamber for a guard, and named after a god. Excavators found thirty-six feet of one gate still stand-

In 586 B.C. Nebuchadrezzar II entered the conquered city of Jerusalem. After looting and burning the city, he exiled most of its citizens to Babylon.

The Shrine atop the Ziggurat

Herodotus described the shrine on the structure he assumed to have been the Tower of Babel and commented on its purpose, as quoted by Georges Roux in Ancient Iraq.

"In the last tower (=storey) there is a great shrine; and in it a great and well-covered couch is laid, and a golden tablet set hard by. But no image has been set up in the shrine, nor does any creature lie therein for the night, except one native woman, chosen from all women by the god, as say the Chaldaeans, who are priests of this god. The same Chaldaeans say—but I do not believe them—that the god himself is wont to visit the shrine and rest upon the couch."

ing. There was a moat around each wall, deep and wide enough to accommodate boats that came off the Euphrates River.

The outer wall, which enclosed Nebuchadrezzar's summer palace and Babylon's suburbs, was fifty-six miles long and thirty-six feet wide; it could accommodate two four-horse chariots going in opposite directions. In the space between the walls, Babylonians built reed huts and mud-brick houses. They planted palm groves and gardens to create a refuge from the inner city, which thrived as a busy and noisy marketplace. Canals cut through the city, which rose up on both sides of the Euphrates.

Streets divided the inner city into eight rectangles. The most important street, Procession Street, began at the Ishtar Gate, ran past the palace and the ziggurat, and turned to cross the river on a bridge built with six boat-shaped piers. Sixty-five feet wide, Procession Street was paved with white limestone and red breccia (rock fragments embedded into a fine-grained substance). Bordering the street was a blue ceramic wall; into this wall, placed in relief at regular intervals, were sixty symbols of Ishtar: lions with red and yellow manes. The Ishtar Gate was faced with the same bright blue enameled bricks. Into it were cast 575 red-and-white relief figures of dragons and bulls, symbolizing Marduk and Adad, the storm god. The Berlin Museum houses a reconstruction of the Ishtar Gate showing its ornamental facade.

Adjoining the Ishtar Gate, Nebuchadrezzar built his city residence to be "the marvel of mankind, the centre of the Land, the shining Residence, the dwelling of Majesty."[45] The palace carried out the same theme, with yellow, white, and red ceramic animals placed in relief on blue enameled bricks. A larger version of the same plan used in older Mesopotamian

As king of Babylon, Nebuchadrezzar II set about making the city the most beautiful ever to exist. At left, a painting shows Babylon as it must have looked during Nebuchadrezzar's reign. At right lie the ruins of the Ishtar Gate, once covered with reliefs of lions, dragons, and bulls.

A reconstruction of the Ishtar Gate is housed in the Berlin Museum. Its tiles are bright blue and are carved with red and white animals symbolic of the gods.

palaces, this one had five courtyards, three entrances, a throne room, reception rooms, royal apartments, storage rooms, and roof gardens, the most famous of the hanging gardens of Babylon. Nebuchadrezzar reportedly built the hanging gardens for one of his wives, Amytis, a princess from the land of the Medes, who was used to lush mountain flowers and trees and hated dry, barren Babylon. Historian Will Durant describes the gardens:

> The topmost terrace was covered with rich soil to the depth of many feet, providing space and nourishment not merely for varied flowers and plants, but for the largest and most deep-rooted trees. Hydraulic engines concealed in the columns and manned by shifts of slaves carried water from the Euphrates to the highest tier of the gardens. Here, seventy-five feet above the ground, in the cool shade of tall trees, and surrounded by exotic shrubs and fragrant flowers, the ladies of the royal harem walked.[46]

The Greek historian Herodotus, who visited Babylon, referred to the city with its walls and hanging gardens as one of the seven wonders of the ancient world.

An artist's version of the hanging gardens of Babylon, said to be one of the seven wonders of the ancient world.

Restoration of Temples and Ceremonies

Babylon's ziggurat, considered the foundation of heaven and earth, was the most famous building rebuilt in the city, similar to the one built by Ur-Nammu during the Third Dynasty of Ur. Rising 650 feet above the ground in seven stages, it had a triple flight of stairs from the ground level and ramps from the second floor up. On top a shrine made with blue enameled bricks contained a solid-gold platform and an ornate bed where a woman slept each night waiting for the god to arrive. This rebuilt ziggurat is thought to be the Tower of Babel, described in a Hebrew story told in the Old Testament. In the biblical story, a primitive people decide to make a name

for themselves by building a tower with its top reaching heaven. To squelch an arrogance that might lead the people to take on God himself, Yahweh causes the tower builders to start speaking many languages. Unable to understand one another, the workers are obliged to stop construction.

Built next to the ziggurat, Babylon's most famous temple, Esagila, was the place where the city-god Marduk dwelled. Nebuchadrezzar said he covered the inner walls of the cella, the room for the statue, with gold to make it shine like the sun. According to Herodotus, the temple had a

> great sitting figure of Marduk, all of gold on a golden throne, supported on a base of gold, with a golden table standing beside it. I was told by the Chaldaeans that to make all this more

Slaves work on the Tower of Babel, which is said to have risen 650 feet off the ground.

At left lie the ruins of Esagila, Babylon's most famous temple and the place where the city's patron god, Marduk (right), dwelled. Marduk, as king of the gods, was the focus of an eleven-day New Year festival, an ancient Sumerian rite reinstated by Nebuchadrezzar.

than 22 tons of gold were used. Outside the temple is a golden altar, and there is another, not of gold, but of great size. . . . On the larger altar the Chaldaeans offer some two and a half tons of frankincense every year at the festival of Bel [Marduk].[47]

Nebuchadrezzar also restored the traditional New Year festival begun centuries earlier in Sumer, believed magically to renew nature and to assure good fortune for the people. Called the *akîtu*, the Babylonian festival was celebrated for eleven days in March or April. The activities of the festival merged magic and reality. People be-

lieved that priests, by using statues, made the activities of the gods actually happen. During the first eight days, symbolizing a period when Marduk was held in the underworld, there were prayers, hymns, meals, readings of the creation story, purification, incantations and burning of incense. They sacrificed a ram, whose body and head, representing the year's sins, were thrown into the river. During these rites, the public mourned. Then the king went ten miles to fetch the god Nabu, who was to deliver Marduk from the underworld. Other gods arrived, and with the king, they performed the rites necessary to bring Marduk back to earth. On the eighth day, Marduk was resurrected and came to the temple, where he met the other gods. In a grand chariot led by the king, Marduk (the statue) rode down Procession Street through the Ishtar Gate amid clouds of incense. There was singing and instrumental music, and the people along the way knelt in adoration. Marduk had triumphed over evil and the gods had returned. After three days, the gods told the destiny of the land. The festival ended with a huge banquet, and people went home hopeful for another year.

Nebuchadrezzar's Babylon

During the first part of Nebuchadrezzar's reign, the economy and social life of the common people resembled conditions of the expansion period in Sumer. During the years of Aramaean invasions, temple lands that had been sold to wealthy families had been transferred back to the temple. Thus, in Nebuchadrezzar's Babylon, the temple was again the social, cultural, and economic center. After a time, however, economic wealth began to decline. Nebuchadrezzar and his father had spent large amounts of money restoring temples, keeping an army, and rebuilding other cities. And tributes were down. Distant cities either were cut off or lacked the wealth to pay. As the capital city used up its financial resources, prices increased and salaries declined, making an unhealthy economy.

Babylon still had not invented coined money, but the old silver system based on weights had been standardized. The standardized system brought with it the idea of credit, which had not been feasible earlier, when rates could not be confirmed. The new system set up a ratio of silver to gold. People with wealth set up private banks and charged 20 to 30 percent interest; as a result, people who had to borrow to survive became enslaved debtors. The development of banking and the depletion of wealth spent on the massive rebuilding brought down the economy and weakened the nation.

Nebuchadrezzar, with his minister Nabonidus, rebuilt temples at Larsa, Kish, and Marad near Nippur, as well as public buildings in several southern cities. In addition, they reconstructed the entire city of Ur, although the rebuilt wall, ziggurat, and monuments had little of the grandeur of the originals from the Third Dynasty period. As the work proceeded, both men, particularly Nabonidus, became interested in excavation. They found many tablets telling about past events in Mesopotamia, including a memorial tablet of Nebuchadrezzar I and a tablet inscribed by Hammurabi. While excavating one of the palaces in Ur, they came across a room containing objects from many places, which they realized was a private museum, kept by a princess named Belshalti-Nannar. Among the exhibits were bricks stamped with the seal of an ancient king and a small, drum-shaped clay object, which turned out to be "the earliest museum label known, drawn up a hundred years before and kept, presumably together with the original bricks, as a record of the first scientific excavations at Ur."[48] The excavation site also produced an ivory cosmetic box, perhaps belonging to the princess. Many of the restoration projects started by the two men were continued by Nabonidus after Nebuchadrezzar's death.

Decline of the Neo-Babylonian Empire

No information remains concerning the last years of Nebuchadrezzar's reign, which ended with the death of the monarch in 562 B.C. The rebuilder of Babylon was succeeded by his son and by an army general, both of whom had brief reigns. Nabonidus (reigned 555–539 B.C.) became the next king, but he made unpopular religious and administrative reforms. In addition, he worshiped the god Sin instead of Marduk and suspended the New Year festival. Instead of ruling the empire, Nabonidus spent his time on archaeological work. Without explanation, he put his son in charge as regent and led an army to northwest Arabia, where he stayed for ten years. Verses in the biblical book of Daniel state that Nebuchadrezzar went mad and lived with beasts, crawling on all fours and eating grass. But the writer was mistaken, according to Georges Roux. The rumor of Nebuchadrezzar's madness originated in stories made up about Nabonidus, whose unconventional interests and allegedly bizarre behavior were considered inappropriate by Babylonian political activists. In "The Verse Account of Nabonidus,"

Mistaken Identity

Thinking that certain false stories (circulated about Nabonidus for political reasons) referred to Nebuchadrezzar, the writer of the biblical book of Daniel used these tales as the basis for his description of Nebuchadnezzar (Nebuchadrezzar) during his last days. This translation of Daniel 4:28–33 is in The New Oxford Annotated Bible.

"All this came upon King Nebuchadnezzar. At the end of twelve months he was walking on the roof of the royal palace of Babylon, and the king said, 'Is this not magnificent Babylon, which I have built as a royal capital by my mighty power and for my glorious majesty?' While the words were still in the king's mouth, a voice came from heaven: 'O King Nebuchadnezzar, to you it is declared: The kingdom has departed from you! You shall be driven away from human society, and your dwelling shall be with the animals of the field. You shall be made to eat grass like oxen, and seven times shall pass over you, until you have learned that the Most High has sovereignty over the kingdom of mortals and gives it to whom he will.' Immediately the sentence was fulfilled against Nebuchadnezzar. He was driven away from human society, ate grass like an oxen, and his body was bathed with the dew of heaven, until his hair grew as long as eagles' feathers and his nails became like birds' claws."

gossips accused this king of being a mad-man, a liar, and a heretic.

After Nebuchadrezzar's lengthy reign, Babylonian power declined and Persian power grew. Persians, who spoke an Indo-European language, had entered what is now Iran at the end of the second millennium, at roughly the same time as the Medes. In 549 B.C., while Nabonidus ruled in Babylon, Cyrus II came to the throne in Persia. Cyrus slowly gained territory and then conquered the Median kingdom. He spent the next ten years on military campaigns that won him the biggest empire the world had ever known. He first went north to Asia Minor and defeated Croesus, the wealthy king of Lydia, and took Ionian cities in Greece. Then he went in the other direction and conquered the present lands of Iran, Turkey, Afghanistan, and part of India. When Nabonidus was in Arabia, Cyrus saw his chance to take what remained of the Babylonian Empire.

Cyrus II came to the throne of Persia in 549 B.C. After amassing the biggest empire the world had ever known, Cyrus cast his eye toward the Babylonian Empire.

The Rise of the Persians Under Cyrus

After seizing cities near the Persian Gulf, Cyrus began a propaganda campaign in Babylon. He tried to win the people's goodwill by posing as a liberator, come to free the captive Hebrews with promises of mercy. In 539 B.C., during the first New Year festival Babylonians had had in many years, Cyrus attacked the city. Other than a battle with Nabonidus's son, Cyrus met little resistance. Herodotus explains the easy takeover by the Persian king:

> As it was, the Persians came upon them [the Babylonians] by surprise and so took the city. Owing to the vast size of the place, the inhabitants of the central parts, as the residents of Babylon declare, long after the outer portions of the town were taken, knew nothing of what had chanced, but as they were engaged in a festival, continued dancing and revelling until they learnt the capture but too certainly.[49]

Cyrus captured the unpopular Nabonidus and had him killed. Then, entering Babylon in triumph, he appointed a Persian governor, ending the last local dynasty ever to rule the city. The following year Cyrus was represented at the New Year festival by his son, a sign that the new Persian rule was legitimate.

Because Cyrus treated Babylonians with respect, he was praised throughout the empire. He brought order by enforcing laws. He reinstated the gods of Sumer

A New King in Babylon

On an inscription on a clay barrel, Cyrus described how he took over Babylon. In Volume I of The Ancient Near East, *anthologist James B. Pritchard includes historian Leo Oppenheim's translation of the inscription. An excerpt describes the first actions Cyrus took as ruler of Babylon.*

"When I entered Babylon (DIN.TIR) as friend and (when) I established the seat of government in the palace of the ruler under jubilation and rejoicing, Marduk, the great lord, [induced] the magnanimous inhabitants of Babylon (DIN.TIR) [to love me], and I was daily endeavouring to worship him. My numerous troops walked around in Babylon (DIN.TIR) in peace, I did not allow anybody to terrorize (any place) of the [country of Sumer] and Akkad. I strove for peace in Babylon (Ka.dingir.ra) and in all his (other) sacred cities. I brought relief to their dilapidated housing, putting (thus) an end to their (main) complaints. Marduk, the great lord, was well pleased with my deeds and sent friendly blessings to myself, Cyrus, the king who worships him, to Cambyses, my son, the offspring of [my] loins, as well as to all my troops, and we all [praised] his great [godhead] joyously, standing before him in peace."

and Akkad in their chapels. He refrained from destroying cities people lived in. He pleased the Hebrews, so long in captivity in Babylon, by freeing them to return to Jerusalem to reestablish their religion there. He pleased the Babylonians by declaring that Marduk was to be worshiped again. An Akkadian clay cylinder describes his popularity:

> All the inhabitants of Babylon, as well as the entire country of Sumer and Akkad, princes and governors, bowed to him (Cyrus) and kissed his feet, jubilant that he had received the kingship, and with shining faces happily greeted him as a master through whose help they had come to life from death and

had all been spared damage and disaster, and they worshipped his name.[50]

Cyrus ruled until his death in 529 B.C., but several Persian kings followed, all attempting to govern humanely by respecting people's gods and promoting equal rights and responsibilities for all. The kings also ensured their financial base by helping their subjects to prosper and taxing them at modest rates.

Darius, Xerxes, and Death

Peaceful times ended in 520 B.C., when Darius I became king of Persia, instituting one set of laws for the entire empire, regardless of local customs. To ensure that Babylonians paid their tributes, Darius divided the kingdom into regions called satrapies and sent tax collectors and royal inspectors called satraps. To unify the empire's monitor system, he changed the base currency, or standard, from silver to gold. Babylonia quietly accepted the changes of Darius, but when Xerxes became king in 485 B.C., Babylonians tried to recover some of their freedom. Xerxes

Darius I (shown with attendants) was less tolerant of local customs than were his predecessors. He instituted a universal set of laws to be observed throughout the entire Persian Empire.

crushed the revolt and tortured and killed many rebels. He damaged people's temples and took the statues of their gods. What was not ruined was left to decay from lack of maintenance. By the end of Xerxes' reign in 465 B.C., no one in Babylon was strong enough to combat Persian repression.

Conditions were bad in Babylon. Overtaxed by a foreign king, the people were also victims of local satraps' greed. One satrap required the taxes of four villages just to feed his dogs. Inflation and unemployment rose. Trade routes no longer ran through the city, and although wages remained the same, rent and the cost of living went up. Moreover, the population had become a mixture of Medes, Arabs, Jews, and Persians, adding other gods and different languages. Since Aramaic, the lingua franca of business and trade, had replaced the Babylonian language, only a small minority could read and write Akkadian and Sumerian in the cuneiform script. Without its language, a nation forgets its past and loses its identity. Archaeologist Georges Roux describes the end:

> The emergence of a monetary system and the development of large-scale banking are phenomena the importance of which cannot be overstressed; but the resurgence of the temples as major social and economic units is equally important. Both help to explain what happened after Babylonia had lost her political autonomy. Economic depression contributed to the decline of the Mesopotamian civilization, but the temples kept it alive for almost 600 years. By a remarkable coincidence, this civilization was to die as it was born: under the wings of the gods.[51]

Xerxes and his queen. Xerxes was even less tolerant of local religion and culture than was his predecessor, Darius. Xerxes put down revolts swiftly and destroyed his subject people's temples and gods.

Woolley's excavations in Ur indicate that the Persians had brought in their own ideas about how to build houses, conduct trade, and worship gods. Nonetheless, the city continued to exist until some time late in the fourth century B.C. Ur did not die from economic decline or invasion; it died because the Euphrates River changed its course. Archaeologist Leonard Woolley explains:

> To-day the Euphrates runs ten miles to the east of the ruins and the great plain is a barren desert. When the river changed its course we do not yet know, but the drying-up of the old bed meant the stoppage of water-borne traffic, the ruin of the whole elaborate system of irrigation, and the end of agriculture; there was not the energy or the capital for the installation of a new system, and the starving city had no longer any reason for existence. Gradually the inhabitants moved away to other homes, the houses crumbled, the winds sweeping across the now parched and desiccated [dried-up] levels brought clouds of sand which they dropped under the lee of the standing walls, and what had been a great city became a wilderness of brick-littered mounds rising from the waste.[52]

Chapter

9 Invasion: Greek Conquest and the End of a Civilization, 331 B.C.

A civilization ends when it has become too weak to defend itself, and invaders come in and take over. In Babylon, the reigns of Darius I and Xerxes were the beginning of the end because the changes made by these rulers—the introduction of the satrap form of organization and the excessive taxation—weakened Babylon beyond recovery. The end came less than a century and a half later. In the interim, the Persian Empire had four kings. By the reign of Persian king Artaxerxes III (358–337 B.C.), Philip II of Greece had unified his forces in Macedonia. Philip was assassinated in 336, and at the age of twenty his son Alexander became king of Macedon. Within two years of assuming the throne, Alexander launched a military campaign that created an empire greater than that of the Persians.

Alexander marched into Asia Minor in 334 B.C. and conquered it. The Persian king Darius III met him in a battle at Issus, just north of Antioch, but Alexander's army was too powerful and Darius fled. Alexander turned south and took Syria and Egypt before he turned to Babylonia. Historian Joan Oates describes the Persian defeat in Babylon:

> In 331 Alexander, having made himself master of the entire eastern

Mediterranean, including Egypt, set forth to do battle with the Persians, led by Darius III (335–331). Advancing with 7000 cavalry and 30,000 infantry Alexander crossed the Euphrates at Thapsacus, on two pontoon bridges. Darius, expecting the Macedonian to

Philip II of Macedon was a fine ruler in his own right but is best known as the father of Alexander the Great.

follow the obvious course down river to Babylon, stationed his troops beyond the upper Tigris whence he could cut off Alexander's line of supply. Alexander outwitted him, however, and moved eastward, crossing the Tigris unopposed above Nineveh. Darius now drew his battle lines at Gaugamela, modern Keramlais, not far east of the Assyrian capital, where the plain had been leveled to permit the Persian chariots to manoeuvre freely. The ensuing struggle was Alexander's, and Darius fled ignominiously [disgracefully], thus bringing to an end the greatest and most efficient imperial organization the ancient world had then known.[53]

After staying in Babylon for a month, sacrificing to Marduk and promising to restore the damage done by Xerxes, Alexander marched through Persia and on to the Ganges River in India. A legend says that he wept when he came to the Ganges because there were no more worlds for him to conquer. He came back to Babylon with grand plans to make Alexandria, in Egypt, and Babylon the twin capitals of his empire. But his plans never materialized, for on June 13, 323 B.C., Alexander, called by then Alexander the Great, died at the age of thirty-three.

The invasion by the Greeks was more than a takeover by new rulers. Mesopotamia, or Babylonia, had been conquered many times, and always the victors had

King Darius and Alexander face off at the Battle of Issus. Alexander defeated Darius's army after Darius fled the scene.

Alexander the Great conquered the Persian Empire.

found the local culture superior and had adopted it. But the Greeks thought differently. When they arrived, the old Mesopotamian culture was little more than a tradition carried on by the temple priests. Literature had lost its liveliness after Hammurabi. Sculpture died with the Assyrians. And architecture still followed the plans created in the ancient cities in Sumer. The tradition that had held together a civilization for more than three thousand years was now a disadvantage. Archaeologist Georges Roux describes the Ancient Near East at the dawn of a new age:

The new world heralded by Alexander was a fast changing world marked by extensive commercial intercourse, bursting with curiosity, eager to reappraise most of its religious, moral, scientific and artistic values. There was no room in such a world for a literature which none but a few scholars could read, for an art which drew its inspiration from outdated ideals and models, for a science which evaded rational explanations, for a religion which did not admit skepticism. The Mesopotamian civilization, like its

Egyptian counterpart, was condemned. If it were permissible to enclose a highly complex phenomenon into one single and necessarily inaccurate formula, one could say that it died of old age.[54]

The Legacy of the First Civilization

By the time it ended, the first civilization of the world had already left its mark on cultures that had adopted its achievements. And the list of achievements is long.

First, Sumer created prototypes (original forms serving as models) for institutions and professions. City-states, like those in Sumeria, arose in the area ranging from the western Mediterranean to India. Sumerians left models for schools and libraries. Today's philosophers, clergy, teachers, historians, poets, lawyers, doctors, reformers, statesmen, politicians, architects, and sculptors perform the same functions as the first professional people in Sumer.

Second, the Sumerians left science, mathematics, and a basic technology. Babylonian medicine paved the way for Hippocrates of Greece. Sumerians left the world the twelve signs of the zodiac, the concept of the calendar and a prototype, and the idea of astronomy. Today we measure a circle, a year, an hour, and a dozen eggs according to their number system. They left the world the principles of agriculture and irrigation; they showed future generations how to make and use drainage systems, the wheel, and the sailing vessel.

Third, Sumerians created the idea of language and law. Their scribes developed practical ways to record business transactions, history, and literature in permanent cuneiform script, which was used through-

The ancient city of Babylon as it may have looked at its height. The ancient Mesopotamians left a prodigious legacy that greatly influenced later civilizations.

out the Ancient Near East. Biblical law, as recorded in the books of Numbers and Deuteronomy in the Old Testament, resembles the legislation of Hammurabi in content and terminology, and Hammurabi's laws resemble Ur-Nammu's laws from the Third Dynasty.

Fourth, Sumerians developed art and architecture. Their sculptors made models of gods and kings and recorded the important events and symbols in sculptured reliefs. Their artists painted murals. Their architects introduced foundations and platforms and made structures of brick. They invented the dome and the arch. Christian churches today have three-sided niches for statues of the saints like the niches for gods in Sumerian temples.

Fifth, Sumerians gave their world and ours religious ideas and literary forms. A thousand years before the Hebrew Bible was written, Sumerian stories told of a world created by divine command, a world begun with the separation of heaven and earth and humans created from clay. Sumerian stories introduced such religious and spiritual concepts as a divine paradise, a survivor of the Flood, a suffering servant of the deity, and a personal god. The Gilgamesh epic led the way for Odysseus and Beowulf. The scribes recorded hymns and proverbs and fables.

Will Durant sums up the legacy of the first civilization:

> Greece did not begin civilization—it inherited far more civilization than it began; it was the spoiled heir of three millenniums of arts and sciences brought to its cities from the Near East by the fortunes of trade and war. In studying and honoring the Near East we [acknowledge] . . . a debt long due to the real founders of European and American civilization. . . . The civilization of the Land between the Rivers passed down into the cultural endowment of our race. In the end nothing is lost.[55]

Notes

Chapter 1: Mixture: The First Farms, 6000–5000 B.C.

1. Georges Roux, *Ancient Iraq.* New York: World, 1964.
2. Carroll Quigley, *The Evolution of Civilizations: An Introduction to Historical Analysis.* New York: Macmillan, 1961.
3. Quigley, *The Evolution of Civilizations.*
4. Roux, *Ancient Iraq.*
5. Roux, *Ancient Iraq.*

Chapter 2: Gestation: The First Cities, 5000–4500 B.C.

6. Quoted in Samuel Noah Kramer, *History Begins at Sumer.* 1956. Reprinted Garden City, NY: Doubleday Anchor Books, 1959. Quotations from the almanac in the next paragraph come from the same source.
7. Samuel Noah Kramer, *The Sumerians: Their History, Culture, and Character.* Chicago: University of Chicago Press, 1963.
8. Quigley, *The Evolution of Civilizations.*
9. Sir Leonard Woolley, *Excavations at Ur.* New York: Crowell, 1965.
10. Woolley, *Excavations at Ur.*

Chapter 3: Expansion: Life and Growth in the City-States, 4500–2500 B.C.

11. Roux, *Ancient Iraq.*
12. Kramer, *The Sumerians.*
13. Quigley, *The Evolution of Civilizations.*
14. Kramer, *The Sumerians.*
15. Quigley, *The Evolution of Civilizations.*
16. Harriet Crawford, *Sumer and the Sumerians.* Cambridge: Cambridge University Press, 1991.
17. Kramer, *The Sumerians.*

Chapter 4: Expansion: Religion and Art of Sumerian Dynasties, 4500–2500 B.C.

18. Roux, *Ancient Iraq.*
19. Roux, *Ancient Iraq.*
20. Quoted in James B. Pritchard, ed., *The Ancient Near East: An Anthology of Texts and Pictures,* 2 vols. 1958. Reprinted Princeton, NJ: Princeton University Press, 1973.
21. Quoted in Kramer, *History Begins at Sumer.*
22. Quoted in Pritchard, *The Ancient Near East.*
23. Quoted in Kramer, *The Sumerians.*
24. Seton Lloyd, *The Archaeology of Mesopotamia: From the Old Stone Age to the Persian Conquest,* rev. ed. 1984. Reprinted London: Thames and Hudson, 1987.
25. Woolley, *Excavations at Ur.*
26. Woolley, *Excavations at Ur.*

Chapter 5: Conflict: Imperial Wars, 2500–800 B.C.

27. Quoted in Roux, *Ancient Iraq.*
28. Woolley, *Excavations at Ur.*
29. Joan Oates, *Babylon,* vol. 94 of *Ancient Peoples and Places,* Glyn Daniel, ed. London: Thames and Hudson, 1979.
30. Roux, *Ancient Iraq.*
31. Quoted in Roux, *Ancient Iraq.*

Chapter 6: Influence and Conflict: Mesopotamia and Its Neighbors, 1750–800 B.C.

32. O. R. Gurney, *The Hittites,* rev. ed. Baltimore: Penguin, 1962.
33. Will Durant, *Our Oriental Heritage,* vol. 1 of *The Story of Civilization.* New York: Simon & Schuster, 1954.

34. Quigley, *The Evolution of Civilizations*.

35. Durant, *Our Oriental Heritage*.

Chapter 7: Universal Empire: The Assyrians, 1600–609 B.C.

36. Woolley, *Excavations at Ur*.

37. Roux, *Ancient Iraq*.

38. Roux, *Ancient Iraq*.

39. Oates, *Babylon*.

40. Quoted in Oates, *Babylon*.

41. Quoted in Quigley, *The Evolution of Civilizations*.

42. Quoted in Roux, *Ancient Iraq*.

43. T. Walter Wallbank and Alastair M. Taylor, *Civilization: Past and Present*, rev. ed., 2 vols. Chicago: Scott, Foresman, 1949.

44. Roux, *Ancient Iraq*.

Chapter 8: Decay: The End of Babylon and Ur, 609–331 B.C.

45. Quoted in Roux, *Ancient Iraq*.

46. Durant, *Our Oriental Heritage*.

47. Quoted in Oates, *Babylon*.

48. Woolley, *Excavations at Ur*.

49. Quoted in Oates, *Babylon*.

50. Quoted in Roux, *Ancient Iraq*.

51. Roux, *Ancient Iraq*.

52. Woolley, *Excavations at Ur*.

Chapter 9: Invasion: Greek Conquest and the End of a Civilization, 331 B.C.

53. Oates, *Babylon*.

54. Roux, *Ancient Iraq*.

55. Durant, *Our Oriental Heritage*.

For Further Reading

Necia H. Apfel, *Calendars: A First Book*. New York: Franklin Watts, 1985. A history of the development of the calendar, from the first farmers who followed the phases of the moon and the establishment of the 365-day year through Egyptian and Roman calendars.

C.W. Ceram, *Gods, Graves, and Scholars: The Story of Archaeology*. Trans. E. B. Garside and Sophie Wilkins. New York: Knopf, 1967. An account of the development of Babylonia, Assyria, and Sumeria with a focus on excavating at Nineveh and deciphering cuneiform. Other chapters on Greece and Egypt.

Jean-Michel Coblence, *The Earliest Cities*. Trans. Anthea Ridett. Morristown, NJ: Silver Burdett, 1987. An easy-to-read account of Jericho and Sumerian cities of Uruk, Ur, and Mari, illustrated with many color pictures of temples, town life, war, and the Flood.

Leila Merrell Foster, *Iraq: Enchantment of the World*. Chicago: Childrens Press, 1990. Beginning with a history of the ancient Sumerian civilization and the influence of Islam, this book also tells about modern Iraq's government, industry, and customs.

Robin Lane Fox, *The Search for Alexander*. Boston: Little, Brown, 1980. A biography of Alexander the Great, well illustrated in color and filled with art and references to heroes and myths of places where Alexander built his empire.

Peter Green, *Alexander of Macedon: A Historical Biography*. Berkeley: University of California Press, 1991. A thorough biography of Alexander beginning with his father, Philip of Macedonia, following Alexander's conquests to the last chapter, "How Many Miles to Babylon?" Maps, many notes and references, and an annotated bibliography.

W. John Hackwell, *Digging to the Past: Excavations in Ancient Lands*. New York: Charles Scribner's Sons, 1986. A short, easy-to-read explanation of archaeological work—how to begin, take notes, sift, and work as a team. Explains the significance of artifacts and findings in tombs.

Steven G. Hyslop, Brian Pobanka, and the editors of Time-Life Books, *Empires Ascendant: Time Frame 400 BC–AD 200*. Alexandria, VA: Time-Life Books, 1987. The first chapter covers Alexander and his conquest of the Ancient Near East.

Elizabeth Lansing, *The Sumerians: Inventors and Builders*, in *Early Culture Series*. Ed. Edward R. Sammis. New York: McGraw-Hill, 1971. A social and cultural history organized by topics such as school, work, law, art, science, and literature. Good photos of artifacts.

James Michael Lynch, ed., and the editors of Time-Life Books, *Sumer: Cities of Eden*. Alexandria, VA: Time-Life Books, 1993. An account of the earliest people, their "milestone" developments, the splendor of kings, and the bloody wars they fought. Wonderful photos, maps, and a timeline.

Edward Rice, *Babylon, Next to Nineveh: Where the World Began*. New York: Four

Winds Press, 1979. A description of the region's geography is followed by a social history of the oldest cities, Sumerian cities, and Babylon. Closes with the conquests that occurred after that of Babylon.

E.A. Speiser, "Mesopotamia: Light That Did Not Fail," in *Everyday Life in Ancient Times: Highlights of the Beginning of Western Civilization in Mesopotamia, Egypt, Greece, and Rome.* Washington, DC: National Geographic Society, 1958. Abundant color illustrations accompany explanations of temples, pottery making, cylinder-seals, royal tombs, the New Year festival, sacrifices, slavery, and law.

Geoffrey Trease, *Hidden Treasure.* New York: Dutton, 1989. A short, easy-to-read book with a chapter on Woolley's excavation of the royal tombs.

H.V.F. Winstone, *Uncovering the Ancient World.* New York: Facts On File, 1985. Organized by excavations, the book has chapters on Nineveh, Mesopotamia, and Babylon. Illustrated with photos and color drawings.

Sir Leonard Woolley, *The Sumerians.* New York: Norton, 1965. Woolley's history telling about the land and early settlers, the kings' list and the Flood, the civil wars, the Third Dynasty of Ur, and the struggles between Isin and Larsa after Ur's destruction. Contains a few black-and-white drawings.

Works Consulted

Guillermo Algaze, "The Uruk Expansion: Cross-Cultural Exchange in Early Mesopotamian Civilization," *Current Anthropology*, December 1989. An archaeologist argues that even in its earliest days, Uruk's lack of natural resources necessitated trade with peripheral states to exchange agricultural products for these natural resources.

Harriet Crawford, *Sumer and the Sumerians*. Cambridge: Cambridge University Press, 1991. A social history that tells about agriculture, town planning, buildings, and beliefs. Well illustrated with diagrams of buildings and drawings of sculpture.

Will Durant, *Our Oriental Heritage*. Vol. 1 of *The Story of Civilization*. New York: Simon & Schuster, 1954. Primarily a social and intellectual history of the Ancient Near and Far East, with sections on Sumeria, Babylonia, the small nations, Judaea, Assyria, and Persia.

The Economist, "Mesopotamian Art: Secrets of Sargon," January 20, 1990. A short report on a new display at the Iraq Museum, showing the jewelry from tombs found during excavations of the palace of Sargon II.

Henry Jackson Flanders Jr., Robert Wilson Crapps, and David Anthony Smith, *People of the Covenant: An Introduction to the Old Testament*. 3rd ed. New York: Oxford University Press, 1988. A thorough account of the ancient Hebrew people as their history is told in the Old Testament. Places the Hebrews' history in the context of the history of the entire Ancient Near East.

O.R. Gurney, *The Hittites*. Rev. ed. Baltimore: Penguin, 1962. A brief chronology of the development of the Hittite Empire, with sections on daily life, law, warfare, religion, language, and art. Includes drawings and photos of artifacts.

Dora Jane Hamblin and the editors of Time-Life Books, *The First Cities*. New York: Time-Life Books, 1973. A brief account of a few ancient sites, like Jericho and Uruk; illustrations suggest daily activities as they may have happened.

Stephen G. Hyslop, Ray Jones, and David S. Thomson, eds., *The Age of God-Kings: Time Frame 3000–1500 B.C.* Alexandria, VA: Time-Life Books, 1987. Brief accounts of Mesopotamia, Egypt, Crete, and Asia with abundant color photos and other illustrations.

Samuel Noah Kramer, *History Begins at Sumer*. 1956. Reprinted Garden City, NY: Doubleday Anchor Books, 1959. Each of twenty-seven chapters discusses a development that occurred first in Sumer. For example, Kramer tells about the first schools, the first case of juvenile delinquency, the first animal fables, the first love song, and the first library catalog system.

———, *The Sumerians: Their History, Culture, and Character*. Chicago: University of Chicago Press, 1963. A social and intellectual history organized by topic (heroes and kings, religion, literature, education, etc.).

Jonathan Norton Leonard and the editors of Time-Life Books, *The First Farmers*. New York: Time-Life Books, 1973. An illustrated explanation of the first agriculture and the domestication of animals in Mesopotamia, showing how the practices also began in Asia and Central America.

Seton Lloyd, *The Archaeology of Mesopotamia: From the Old Stone Age to the Persian Conquest.* Rev. ed. 1984. Reprinted London: Thames and Hudson, 1987. A book organized according to the chronology of events in Mesopotamia, but focused on artifacts found at important excavation sites. Well illustrated with diagrams and photos.

Joan Oates, *Babylon.* Vol. 94 of *Ancient Peoples and Places.* Ed. Glyn Daniel. London: Thames and Hudson, 1979. A history of Babylon from the days of Hammurabi through the invasion by Alexander, telling about the rulers, the social life of the people, and the artistic, architectural, and literary achievements of each period.

A. Leo Oppenheim, trans., *Letters from Mesopotamia: Official, Business, and Private Letters on Clay Tablets from Two Millennia.* Chicago: University of Chicago Press, 1967. After a long introduction giving a survey of Mesopotamian civilization and explaining the process of translating, the translator presents letters about individual, state, and military matters, most of them sent to leaders by their administrative and household staffs.

James B. Pritchard, ed., *The Ancient Near East: An Anthology of Texts and Pictures.* 2 vols. 1958. Reprinted Princeton, NJ: Princeton University Press, 1973. An anthology of translated texts from the Egyptians, Mesopotamians, Hittites, Canaanites, Assyrians, and Palestinians. It includes myths, laws, historiography, hymns, and letters. Pictures show artifacts found in each nation.

————, *The Ancient Near East: A New Anthology of Texts and Pictures.* 2 vols. Princeton, NJ: Princeton University Press, 1975. An anthology with organization and content like the earlier volume, but with different texts and photos.

Carroll Quigley, *The Evolution of Civilizations: An Introduction to Historical Analysis.* New York: Macmillan, 1961. The author's theory of how civilizations rise and fall is applied to Mesopotamian, Canaanite, Minoan, Classical, and Western civilizations.

Georges Roux, *Ancient Iraq.* New York: World, 1964. A thorough history of Mesopotamia, beginning with a search for the first settlers and ending with the death of the civilization. Emphasis on the leaders and dynasties. Includes photos, charts, and maps.

T. Walter Wallbank and Alastair M. Taylor, *Civilization: Past and Present.* Rev. ed. 2 vols. Chicago: Scott, Foresman, 1949. A general survey of world history, beginning with prehistoric humans and early societies and civilizations.

Sir Leonard Woolley, *Excavations at Ur.* New York: Crowell, 1965. A report on the excavations carried out by the British Museum and the University Museum of Pennsylvania, explaining how excavators dug, where they dug, and what they found. Woolley also comments on the civilization and explains the reasoning for his conclusions.

Index

Picture Credits

Cover photo by Stock Montage

Ancient Art & Architecture Collection, 21, 26, 27, 28, 30, 31, 39 (both), 41, 42 (both), 43, 49 (both), 50 (left), 51 (all), 53, 55, 59, 63, 64, 84

Art Resource, NY, 100

The Bettmann Archive, 22, 37 (both), 46, 54, 58, 65, 69 (both), 72, 76 (bottom), 78, 81, 87, 88 (left), 89, 95, 99 (both), 101 (both), 102 (both), 105, 109, 111

Sonia Halliday Photographs, 71 (top)

Stock Montage, 16, 18, 23, 76 (top), 88 (right), 98, 107, 108, 110, 112

UPI/Bettmann Newsphotos, 14

Werner Forman/Art Resource, NY, 32, 48, 50 (right), 73, 86, 91, 94 (both)

Werner Forman Archive, Schimmel Collection, NY/Art Resource, NY, 71 (bottom)

About the Author

After many years of teaching composition and British literature, Clarice Swisher now devotes her time to research and writing. She is the author of *The Beginning of Language, Relativity, The Importance of Pablo Picasso,* and *The Importance of Albert Einstein.* She lives in Saint Paul, Minnesota.